For the Knowledge of the Glory of the Lord

Regnum Practitioner Series

While we delight to serve the academic community, our mission is to enable the global church to engage more readily in God's mission in its very diverse contexts. To do this we seek to bring practitioners and academics together. Our desire is that this series will bridge the gap that sometimes exists between, on the one hand, Christian leaders and mission practitioners and, on the other, Christian researchers.

FOR THE KNOWLEDGE OF THE GLORY OF THE LORD

CELEBRATING 40 YEARS OF GOD'S MISSION THROUGH THE OXFORD CENTRE FOR MISSION STUDIES

Edited by
David Emmanuel Singh and
Paul Bendor-Samuel

First published 2023 by Regnum Books International

Regnum is an imprint of the Oxford Centre for Mission Studies
St. Philip and St. James Church, Woodstock Road, Oxford, OX2 6HR, UK
www.regnumbooks.net

British Library Cataloguing in Publication Data
A catalogue record for this book is available from the British Library

ISBN: 979-8-8898-3313-0
eBook ISBN: 979-8-8898-3314-7

Typeset in Palatino by WORDS BY DESIGN

Cover image Greg Rakozy www.unsplash.com

Distributed by Fortress Press in the US, Canada, India, and Brazil

regnum

CONTENTS

FOREWORD

HAZEL ANDERSON

The origins of this unique institution lie in the vision, commitment and tenacity of a small number of Christian men and women who were determined to encourage the equal influence and participation of the Two Thirds World Church in the work and witness of the church worldwide. This meant gaining the attention and respect of the church in Europe and North America by establishing networks of theologians and mission workers from the growing Christian Churches in Asia, Africa and Latin America to advocate new perspectives in academic thinking and mission practice.

The Consultation on World Evangelisation (COWE) at Pattaya, Thailand in June 1980 paved the way for a meeting in Cuernavaca, Mexico, in January 1981, to discuss the way forward for 'wholistic mission from bases in each of the six continents'. The statutes of Partnership in Mission, drafted and agreed at the meeting, were the result, giving rise to the establishment of INFEMIT (the International Fellowship of Evangelical Mission Theologians) in 1982 and OCMS (the Oxford Centre for Mission Studies) in 1983.

OCMS was to be and remains the institution where theologians and mission practitioners from the Two Thirds World Church can study and obtain research degrees from accredited British universities and academic bodies. Their studies and research continue to be carried out largely in the countries where they live and work, with annual visits to OCMS for personal contact with supervisors and tutors for a minimum of six weeks. A paradigm for this method of study already existed in TAFTEE (The Association for Theological Education by Extension), founded in India in 1971. Two of the founders of OCMS, Vinay Samuel and Christopher Sugden, had been closely involved with the work of TAFTEE in Bangalore, India, up to 1982. At the same time, their involvement with EFICOR (the Evangelical Fellowship of India Commission on Relief) was bound up with their commitment to a wholistic Christian mission.

OCMS started life in a small office in the then Westminster College in west Oxford manned by Christopher Sugden as Registrar and David Cook as Dean of Studies, who developed the staged research programme still followed by our students today. It became increasingly obvious that a permanent home for the new centre was needed. From his office window, Christopher Sugden could see the steeple of SS Philip and James Church, which was made redundant as a church building in 1982 by the Diocese of Oxford. Initially, OCMS acquired the building for a peppercorn rent before proceeding to outright purchase. Development of the building's interior and the establishment of the library were aided by generous donations from the Lutheran Church in Germany.

Although the main academic emphasis of OCMS has always been its PhD programme, there have been many initiatives in taught diploma and master's courses in-house, in other academic institutions and in partnership with Christian organisations. These are well documented in the OCMS library and archive. The impetus to expand and develop studies in mission continues today in the Guided Research Programme (GRP) and Integrated Mission Leadership (IML).

From the very beginning of its existence, advocacy and publishing were established as core activities of OCMS. Vinay Samuel, for INFEMIT, and Christopher Sugden, for OCMS, were active in attending international conferences to promote a wholistic mission and theological education as well as holding summer and winter schools and study days at OCMS.

The publishing arm of OCMS consists of Regnum Books and *Transformation* journal. Regnum Books was established in the UK in December 1984 and continues to publish a wide range of books on Christian mission by academics and practitioners. The first issue of *Transformation* journal had already appeared in 1983 under the title *Transformation: An International Dialogue of Evangelical Social Ethics*, printed by the Paternoster Press in England. Compiled and edited in-house at OCMS since its inception, it is now published by OCMS in association with Sage Publishing.

We are grateful that on this fortieth anniversary, there are still founders of OCMS here to witness its beginnings and to take pride in the institution it has become.

Hazel Anderson
OCMS Archivist

CHAPTER 1

CONTEXT, INDIVIDUAL LIVES AND THE BEGINNINGS

VINAY SAMUEL

Any history of an institution in which one is involved from conception to establishment for over two decades inevitably becomes a personal story. This is not a story written by an objective historian examining documents and conducting interviews. It cannot be an objective account. It is my story. My justification for sharing this story as history is that there is no other way that I can recount the history of the Oxford Centre for Mission Studies (OCMS). It is not only my story but also the story of a number of others who were there from the beginning. Their stories may differ in marginal details but will not diverge far from the way I recount it.

FRAMING THE CONTEXT

The story of OCMS needs to be framed in its times and context. What OCMS was doing as a post-colonial and decolonised institution was not unique and was not on its own. It was part of what God was doing in history, globally. God was at the heart of large Christian movements such as the Reformation, the Wesleyan Revival, Pentecostalism, and many others. God raises up people, stimulates new ideas, develops old patterns and enables his people to relate to contemporary forces. I see the start of OCMS against the background of the global movements in the last half of the twentieth century and how these movements shaped the individuals who established OCMS.

The generation who founded OCMS grew up after the Second World War. The cultural forces at the time shaped them. As colonialism was being dismantled, the fifties were a decade of freedom. The war had been fought to defend freedom and democracy. Nations that had been colonised got the message and fought for their freedom, which was given sometimes freely and sometimes reluctantly after a struggle. The idea of freedom was crucially important for those of us who were teenagers through this time. Post-colonial states such as India, Pakistan, Nigeria, Kenya, Uganda and Malaysia were free to reconstruct their own identities. Freedom meant we could define our own distinctiveness, govern ourselves and build a future for ourselves. We emerged from the imposed sense of the colonised to a new collective identity.

In such a context, I was not just a citizen of a Muslim princely state (Hyderabad Deccan); I was Indian. From a Christianity received from the West, those of us who were Christian began to discover our own distinctiveness in our national contexts. There was a sense of freedom, which shaped all our activities. We also realised that we needed to build all of this into institutions. The institution building was, therefore, part of our vision of expressing our new identity.

The sixties were a time of cultural upheaval as Western cultures were transforming themselves. Liberalism was prevailing in per sonal, private and public aspects of societies. Some abandoned religious certainties that had underlain societal order, and uncritically embraced anything new. However, colonialism had not ended. The United States, the 'arsenal of freedom and democracy,' found space to impress its desired vision of the world on the whole world. Alongside this, Christian mission found it had space to expand. Biblically-based Christianity, which was declining in what had been its homelands, now found it had space in the rest of the world. Large, well-funded Christian and humanitarian organisations were formed to promote what the world should look like; for example, World Vision, the Billy Graham Evangelistic Association and the Ford Foundation. This version of freedom and democracy could potentially sweep the non-Western world. The challenge was how to defend ourselves from the recurrence of Western colonial hegemony of ideas, ideologies and culture coming from outside our regions. Capitalism and communism were clashing on the global stage and each was trying to co-opt our newly free nations into their values. The non-aligned movement, associated with Jawaharlal Nehru, the Indian Prime Minister, was saying, 'We need our own identity.' Christians were also challenged with the question, 'What kind of faith is ours?'

The seventies was the decade of the Cold War at its height. The world was divided into two camps led respectively by the USA and Russia. Programmes from the USA were developed for the whole world such as the Peace Corps of volunteers. In this decade, Western mission movements grew with the associated ideology. The Church Growth Movement emerged from the USA and firmly rejected any necessary involvement of social action with mission which was equated with evangelism without remainder. Any push in the direction of social action was branded as communism. The approach of some nineteenth century mission groups was being revived, now being supported by international mission organisations backed by huge finances and related institutions. The Berlin Congress on Evangelism of 1966, sponsored by the Billy Graham Organisation (note the venue at the frontier of the clash of ideologies), was followed by the Lausanne Congress on World Evangelisation in 1974. All these forces were continuing to impose what the world, mission and Christianity should look like.

There came, however, a clear pushback at Lausanne. Rene Padilla, a senior leader in the International Fellowship of Evangelical Students from Argentina, had been shaped in the sixties. The sixties had seen the rise of liberation theology which brought in the ideas of 'the centre and the periphery,' 'systemic sin,' 'priority of the poor' and the notion that the gospel of Jesus transformed the whole of life. Vatican II had encouraged this, not crushed it. This enabled Rene Padilla to try to bring its biblical ideas into the evangelical movement. These ideas were expressed in the resistance and pushback from very weak forces and were encapsulated in the radical discipleship statement, which asserted a wholistic understanding of mission embracing both evangelism and social action. The framers of the statement believed that there would be evangelical spaces for this wholistic understanding of mission to flourish. This battle over the understanding and practice of biblically faithful mission was the crucible for founding the International Fellowship of Evangelical Mission Theologians[1] (INFEMIT) and OCMS.

The eighties saw the predicted collapse of the Russian Empire and the emergence of the unipolar world of Francis Fukuyama's *End of History*; freedom, democracy and capitalism were the only future for the world. Those who had resisted the understanding of mission that went with this cultural dominance at Lausanne had no other resources than their intellectual and spiritual gifts. Our writings, fellow scholars and our spiritual energy together forged a common solidarity of purpose. This confidence in the 'triumph of democracy and freedom' was also expressed in a deliberate pushback against the development of wholistic mission in the calling of the Consultation on World Evangelisation (COWE) at Pattaya, Thailand in 1980, at which Billy Graham said the aim was 'to get back to evangelism.' This was an attempt to reverse the understanding of mission, which emerged in the radical discipleship statement at Lausanne. The congress statement adumbrated this reversal and John Stott endorsed it. In response, our group produced the statement of concerns. We realised that colonialism was not dead but was pushing back in neo-colonialism. This statement prompted Stanley Mooneyham, the Chair of the consultation and head of World Vision International to describe us as dangerous enemies of evangelicalism today. This statement gathered the non-Western Christian leadership together who met following the consultation to prepare for action. We realised that we had to build our own

[1] Later to become the International Fellowship of Mission as Transformation.

institutions and networks and not rely on these global organisations and conferences. Out of this came INFEMIT, the process that led to the statement 'Social Transformation: The Church in Response to Human Need' from Wheaton in June 1983, and the vision to train our next generation of leaders.

The nineties saw a consolidation of these resources, as those engaged in mission activity on the ground – bishops, pastors and development workers – demonstrated both an intellectual depth to their activities grounded in a definite biblical theology and an understanding of economics and social reality. They could show practical evidence of how this worked out in mission action through micro-enterprise development, wholistic Christian communities among the poor, and social activism. These were not administrative officers of organisations or isolated academics. Together, this network developed transformational mission and theology.[2] There was still a great deal of colonialism in the academy. Creating space in the Western academy became very important for us to decolonise minds, theology and culture. We did not try to create an alternative space elsewhere. We drew on resources of the academy to develop our own decolonised space in the heart of one of the leading universities in the Western world. The 'nineties' and 'noughties' (2000s) saw two decades of the growth and influence of this mission understanding such that it was regarded as normal, mainstream and taken for granted. The confidence to resist the cultural hegemony of the West remained in our DNA.

OCMS was not alone in how it began during these decades but was part of what God was doing all over the world as he was at work everywhere. God brought together a bishop in Bali, Indonesia; a bishop (eventually an archbishop in Kenya); a businessman in Australia; a student minister in Argentina; a theologian in Ghana; and a bishop in Pakistan who took forward the resistance evidenced in the radical discipleship statement at Lausanne in 1974. All this

[2] See, for example, Mission as Transformation, edited by Samuel and Sugden, Regnum 1999.

resistance to the dominance of the West in culture and theology gave people the confidence to push back against these forces backed by money, organisations and communications to take on other expressions of Western attempts at hegemony. One example was the Lambeth Conference of 1998, where Global South bishops resisted the attempt by the Episcopal Church of the USA to give the sanction of Lambeth to same-sex relationships. The result was the resolution Lambeth 1.10, which remains the standard for Orthodox Anglican understanding of sexuality to this day. In 2003, when the LGBT agenda surfaced again with the proposal for a gay bishop in the Diocese of Oxford, Chris Sugden was released from OCMS to set up with the same network a resistance based on biblical orthodoxy, which resulted in the Archbishop of Canterbury asking the candidate to withdraw. When a gay bishop was consecrated in the USA, archbishops from the Global South called the first Global Anglican Futures Conference (GAFCON) in Jerusalem in 2008. Many Orthodox Christian leaders in the West appeared to lack the ability to resist the cultural forces swamping their own churches or to resist the imperialism being exported to the rest of the world.

GOD'S WORK IN INDIVIDUAL LIVES

Inductive Bible Study

The forces and influences that led to the foundation of OCMS have roots in my own personal journey to the foundation of TAFTEE in India. As an English Literature student at Osmania University, Hyderabad in 1962, I learnt to look carefully at texts. John Ruskin's famous *Essay on Composition* taught me to look at patterns in texts. I then applied this to the text of the Bible. In 1964, I enrolled for Bachelor of Divinity studies at Union Biblical Seminary (UBS), Yavatmal near Nagpur in Central India. In my first week of classes, Kenneth Bauman, the Principal, introduced me to two books: Howard. T. Kuist on *Inductive Bible Study*, and Robert Traina's *Methodical Bible Study*. They were two Presbyterian scholars from Princeton Seminary. I took to inductive study of the Bible like a duck to water. The method focused on looking in the texts at contrasts, comparisons, characters, terms used and words that are stressed. Most importantly, the text could be studied on its own, not least as it was God's Word. This is, of course, the evangelical understanding of scripture which is not just determined by what the reader makes of it (reader-response), or its re-interpretation in a new 'modern' context. This approach attracted me to UBS.

In 1967, I was ordained as an associate pastor at St John's Church Bangalore. This is an English-speaking former Anglican church of the Church of South India with an evangelical tradition. The congregation was full of Indian professionals, doctors, engineers, young working people and college students. I found they were all hungry to study God's Word. One of the problems in the churches of India was that there were many able pastors but they were trained in the seminaries to pastor and teach rather than to train the people of God after the manner of Ephesians 4. 11–13:

> *11 Christ himself gave the apostles, the prophets, the evangelists, the pastors and teachers, 12 to equip his people for works of service, so that the Body of Christ may be built up 13 until we all reach unity in the faith and in the knowledge of the Son of God and become mature, attaining to the whole measure of the fullness of Christ.*

I started training well-educated lay people in the inductive Bible study methodology. I was able to start twelve Bible study groups at St John's led by those trained in inductive Bible study. As will become clear, the place of local churches was central in the beginning, as was growth of Theological Education by Extension (TEE) in India and the development of lay-led church bible study groups. I was able to facilitate the training of lay leaders in the Centenary Methodist Church Hyderabad, which was the home church in my youth. Vinay Moses who grew up with me in that church was the pastor there.

In June 1969, I returned to UBS as Registrar at the age of twenty-seven. In March 1969, Ralph Winter in UBS conducted the first workshop that introduced TEE to India. I was not in post then, but UBS took TEE up as it realised that it would enable learning of the Bible by many more people than those who could study at seminaries. UBS recognised that theological education could be extended to people in their local churches and the seminary could resource such learning. When I started working in UBS from June 1969, Bruce Nicholls, a Bible Medical Missionary Society (BMMF – later to become Interserve) missionary became a champion of TEE and asked me to participate in the discussions about UBS promoting TEE in India as an extension programme of theological education. Bruce was able to get the BMMF to take up TEE as their key ministry.

Key Ingredients

I was at the next TEE consultation in UBS in 1970 but did not become part of the committee. I was released for fifty per cent of the time by the UBS Board to begin setting up TEE groups in the cities of Bombay, Hyderabad and Bangalore. In Bombay, I took TEE to other big English-speaking churches: the Taylor Memorial Methodist Church and Bowen Memorial Methodist Church. Brian Ringrose of BMMF and Chris Wigglesworth of the Church of Scotland, both based in Bombay, also became strong supporters. Ram Dutt Joshi, the United Methodist Church Bishop of Bombay became an enthusiastic supporter. It was amazing to see that the church leadership recognised this as meeting an essential need of the Indian church. Our first course was the Inductive Study of Mark's Gospel. I trained the pastors to lead the groups and visited each group in the three cities at least twice a month.

A BMMF missionary in Madras (Chennai), Ian McCleary, was released to develop TEE groups in Madras and Vellore. Ian went to St John's Church Vellore, another large local English-speaking church, and developed groups in the Church and the medical college. All these churches had lay people who were desperate to be trained in reading and using the Bible for ministry. Senior leaders of the Churches backed us, such as Eric Nasir (CNI Bishop of Nagpur), Maqbul Caleb (the CNI Bishop of Delhi), and Pritam Santaram (a bishop in Delhi and formerly Principal of Bishops College, Calcutta).

In this background, the key ingredients that went into the beginnings of The Association for Theological Education by Extension (TAFTEE) were as follows:

1. The resources and inspiration of inductive Bible study methods;
2. Professional lay people hungry for biblical study and training in ministry with large local churches as bases;
3. Senior leaders committed to seeing this start;
4. Missionaries who found something new to get on with; and
5. UBS recognising that theological training can be extended beyond seminary walls to reach churches in context.

I organised the first committee and requested my dear friend, Sundar Clarke, who at that time was pastor of St Mark's Church, Bangalore (CSI) and later became Bishop of Madras, to take up the role of Chairman. I worked on the documents to register TAFTEE as an association in March 1971. In August 1971, I had to leave for Cambridge UK for my postgraduate studies.

Struggle to Survive

I returned in March 1975 to find TAFTEE about to close with no money and little support. Saphir Athyal who took over as Chair from Sundar Clarke felt UBS could no longer underwrite the budget of TAFTEE. It is probable that UBS, like other seminaries at the time, realised that this new approach was a serious competitor to them. Saphir asked me to take over and do what I could with it. There was only a small amount of money in the TAFTEE account (about £250 at the time). I took over as Chairman and provided leadership for twenty-eight years. In the first eight years, I was responsible for raising all of TAFTEE's funds.

I drew on missionaries, as we could not pay Indian staff. We had a very committed team of BMMF missionaries. I was able to invite the Church Mission Society (CMS) UK and BMMF UK missionaries to join TAFTEE. We did not have to pay them anything and they were a great group. Robin Thompson had learnt programming and taught the team how to do it, and we took off developing our own study material. CMS made Mike Butterworth available in 1977 from his lectureship at the United Theological College (UTC) Bangalore to be the director. Chris Sugden was released by the Bible Churchmen's Missionary Society (BCMS) to join us in 1978 and our focus on contextualisation and wholistic theology took off. It was a period of much innovation for us as we sought to develop study material for labourers with a few years of education through to medical doctors and college professors.

The period from 1975 to 1978 was the struggle to survive. Study by Extension for All Nations (SEAN) from Latin America made their programme, the 'Life of Jesus', available for us. In our struggle for money, BMMF suggested that I undertake a promotional tour, which they sponsored to share TAFTEE's vision and needs with friends in the United States and the UK. In the USA, I visited Menlo Park Presbyterian Church; University Presbyterian Church, Seattle; Bel Air Presbyterian Church in Los Angeles; and the Partnership in Mission Organisation in Pennsylvania. We were able to secure pledges totaling $40,000 a year for three years in 1978. In 1980, I made another such trip to Germany to the Evangelical Lutheran Church of Wurttemberg and Evangelisches Misionswerk in Hamburg, and received substantial support.

Wholistic Mission

A further element had entered TAFTEE's DNA by this time, which made it very attractive to these donors. From my youth, as I tried to share the gospel, I was deeply saddened to see in our rural churches, Christians of the third and fourth generation from the mass movements. When I returned from Cambridge in 1975, I came back with a wholistic understanding of gospel ministry in response to the challenge of poverty and the need to equip the whole people of God for such wholistic mission. Thus, there was a missiological background to the development of TAFTEE's courses. The Lausanne Congress of 1974 had validated the place of social action along with evangelism in the mission of the Church. Chris Sugden joined TAFTEE as a course writer in 1978 and subsequently as Director of Course Writing. He had studied Liberation Theology for his UK Master's degree, written a book called *Social Gospel or No Gospel,* and been commissioned to write a book on radical discipleship, following the Lausanne Conference to flesh out the radical discipleship statement produced at that conference.

In 1969, there was no course at any Indian seminary on Church and Society, Church and State, Human Rights, or Poverty. Yet these were key issues. In 1970, I developed a course on Church and Society for Batchelor of Divinity students at UBS. The Lausanne Congress opened the door for evangelicals to explore these issues from a biblical standpoint. This wholistic understanding meant we created TAFTEE courses on topics that were not in the curricula of theological colleges. The rise of liberation, black and feminist theologies underscored the place of context in theological study, reflection and mission action. These developments explain the expansion of courses from 1978 onwards on Jesus the Liberator, Poverty and Development, The Gospel to the Whole Person, and Working Together for Health. TAFTEE was not just 'extending' seminary courses, it was creating completely new material. The German churches were very excited by this dimension of TAFTEE's work.

These TAFTEE courses were used by the training unit of EFICOR (Evangelical fellowship of India Commission on Relief), which began life in the choir vestry of St John's Church, Bangalore in 1980, and subsequently used by World Vision and other agencies in staff workshops on biblically based, wholistic ministry and mission in development. Together with Chris Sugden, I did a similar workshop in Nepal with the United Mission to Nepal, the one agency allowed in Nepal. We also did a workshop in Bangladesh with World Vision. This was the background to them taking up TAFTEE.

Educational Validation

A further area to be considered is how TAFTEE related to existing frameworks for validating and accrediting theological education in India. TAFTEE was invited to be part of the Board of Theological Education of Serampore College (University) from 1978, and I represented it on the Board from 1978 to 1988. Many residential theological colleges of Serampore seemed to be suspicious and distrusted what they saw as competition. The fact that TAFTEE was evangelical in its Christian position did not help. Both the UTC and the Christian Institute for the Study of Religion and Society, headed by M.M. Thomas, based not far from TAFTEE's head office in Bangalore, spoke against it on the Board. It fell to me to respond to their charges. The first charge was that TAFTEE recruited people who lacked academic quality. My response was that the people studying the courses were the brightest and best of the Indian church, including some professors of medicine at Vellore Medical College. In fact, those studying in the colleges tended to be people who could not get jobs anywhere else. The second charge was that TAFTEE was evangelical in theology. M.M. Thomas maintained this charge until he came to lecture in the TAFTEE/Oxford University MTh course (in Oxford) years later. He acknowledged that this was what theological education should be all about.

Contextualisation

One of TAFTEE's strengths was that the courses, students and tutors all were immersed in and developed out of ministry in the Indian context. From 1975, I had discovered the importance of contextualisation. I gave the Bombay Urban and Industrial League for Development (BUILD) lectures titled 'The Meaning and Cost of Discipleship'. In 1978, I became a co-editor of the International Journal,

Gospel in Context, published by Partnership in Mission in the USA. The Lausanne Movement held a consultation on Gospel and Culture in Bermuda in 1978. The Board of Theological Education at Serampore was astonished by how contextual the content and process of TAFTEE was. All TAFTEE deans and tutors were involved in pastoral ministry. Few teachers from the Serampore affiliated colleges lived in the Indian reality. Interestingly, most of the students at one of the colleges headed by one of our strongest critics, Russell Chandran (Principal of UTC Bangalore), attended St John's Church on Sundays. To his credit, twenty years later he changed his mind and supported the work.

Developments in Postgraduate Study

The missiological debate also was the background to further developments of TEE. Samuel Escobar and Rene Padilla of the Latin American Theological Fraternity pioneered the radical discipleship statement at Lausanne in 1974. In a way, this was a response to the development of liberation theology and a commitment to root social concern for the poor in a biblical understanding. This was discussed further at the follow-up to Lausanne at the Congress on World Evangelisation in Thailand in 1980. Out of this came INFEMIT, a network in Africa, Asia and Latin America. I was the first General Secretary of this network and led it for twenty-five years. Among other issues, the first gathering addressed the question of developing and training a new generation of mission theologians from the Global South who would remain in their countries for their ministry. The problem was that seventy per cent of those who went to the UK and the USA for further studies never returned – their reasons were understandable since they often had school age children for whom free education and posts in the West were most attractive. The solution was to extend TEE to postgraduate PhD degrees so that students would not be required to move west with their families. This was quite logical since PhD degrees did not depend so much on face-to-face input. It was also right for those involved in TAFTEE to take this forward since the DNA had to be suitable to extend the TEE concept and process to postgraduate study successfully.

David Cook, who was involved in the Council of National Academic Awards (CNAA –the precursor to the Open University in the UK) was at the 1980 gathering in Thailand. He put us fully in the picture as to how this could be achieved. The INFEMIT group decided to set up a centre in Oxford to pioneer this, and commissioned Chris Sugden and me to develop a postgraduate academic programme in Oxford that would have distance learning at its centre. Chris left India and returned to Oxford to begin the process. This was the origin of OCMS, which began in 1983. Between then and 2003 we graduated fifty PhD students from four UK university bodies. The candidates spent six weeks per year in Oxford. This meant that their academic and residence costs were greatly reduced. It also meant their families did not come with them, so almost all returned to their own countries. Among OCMS graduates is a bishop in north Myanmar, the presiding bishop of four thousand Pentecostal churches in Africa, the pastor of the leading Pentecostal Church in Calcutta, and many others in senior positions.

Once the PhD programme at Oxford was embedded – first with the CNAA, then the Open University and finally the University of Wales – OCMS developed its master's programme. The Westminster MTh programme in Applied Theology was further revised and offered as an international programme with TAFTEE in India. The MA in World Christianity came later with the University of Oxford, which was handed on to become the TAFTEE/OU masters programme. The same happened with the PhD, where TAFTEE developed a PhD programme with the University of Wales. Topics covered in PhD theses done at OCMS included 'Christian Discipleship Training as a Remedy for the Spread of HIV Aids in Zambia'; 'Justice in Post-Apartheid Namibia'; 'Addressing Corruption in the Church in Nigeria'; and 'Church and State Relations in South Sudan.'

Thus, TEE has fed back into the practice of a university department. Professional lay people, hungry for biblical study and training in ministry, developed a programme inspired by Bible study methods. This programme began initially by offering a certificate course in theology to labourers, farmers, development workers, doctors and professors in India. This was based initially in large local churches and was supported by senior leaders and missionaries. The pastors of these churches had found something new to get on with, and were expressing a wholistic and contextual approach to mission. It continued in partnership with Oxford University and the University of Wales to offer postgraduate degrees, and was the seedbed for not only OCMS but later for the Oxford Centre for Religion in Public Life postgraduate extension education programmes with two South African renowned universities.

OCMS' Beginnings from 1983

Location

Oxford was selected as a location for a number of reasons. Chris Sugden had roots in Oxford, both in the university and with local churches, having studied there from 1966 to 1972. David Cook, a Baptist based in Westminster College, Oxford, a Methodist Foundation, was pioneering postgraduate research degrees by extension with CNAA in 1981. This was very exciting as we considered how to train our young Indian academics. I met Cook at a consultation on Social Ethics at High Leigh in Hoddesdon in 1978. He shared what he was experimenting with; his idea and the support from Westminster were most important. In 1983, I met the Principal, Kenneth Wilson, who was very positive about the vision of OCMS and very hospitable. OCMS' first office was in the college. Westminster College thus provided a basis and home for establishing OCMS and so with such a base, I could begin to ask for funds.

A meeting was held in July / August 1983 at No 1 Five Mile Drive, Oxford at the home of Mrs Hare[3] where a decision was made to set up a mission research institution. The name was chosen as the Oxford Centre for Mission Studies. We decided on Chris Sugden's and David Cook's roles. My role as General Secretary was to make sure it happened. We agreed also that the centre was to use the distance learning approach that I was involved with in India from 1971, and would draw on the model developed by David Cook at Westminster College, Oxford under CNAA and the Open University.

Earlier, I had met with Barry White, Principal of Regent College and Chair of the Theology Faculty Board at Oxford University, who gave his enthusiastic support, as did the Principal of Westminster College and the Vice Chair of the Faculty Board, Kenneth Wilson. Both were evangelicals and keen that something such as our proposal would be essential for Oxford. The most enthusiastic supporter was Bishop Stephen Neil based at Wycliffe at the time who was ready to commend the effort to anyone.

The beginnings go back to the first INFEMIT Conference on Christology in Bangkok in 1982. I invited David Cook to the conference where he presented the Westminster College model. The conference suggested that I work with David and Chris to develop a research centre for equipping non-Western evangelical scholars with postgraduate qualifications. Chris Sugden had worked with me in Bangalore from September 1978 to help develop course material for the new TAFTEE BTh programme, and helped me with the training centre of EFICOR that I started in 1977. We trained community development workers and produced material on the theology of development for the evangelical community. Chris moved to Oxford in May 1983. As a BCMS / Crosslinks missionary,

---

[3] Mrs Hare, a generous and hospitable American widow who settled in Oxford, was a 'grand dame' of St Ebbe's Church who kept open house for graduate Christian students at her home. Her two daughters married and served in Kenya and Pakistan.

he was eligible for six months' salary in the UK, from June to December 1983. We agreed that Partnership in Mission Asia (PIM Asia) would ensure his salary from 1984 as he worked on the research centre project.

As an organisation, it was PIM Asia that resourced/financed the founding of OCMS. It was formed in November 1978 in Manila and connected with the Latin American Theological Fraternity (LATF/FTL) in 1980 at the Lausanne Conference Consultation on World Evangelisation, Bangkok. At Bangkok, it was agreed to organise a gathering in Mexico in 1981. It was resourced/financed by PIM Asia and jointly organised by FTL and PIM Asia. INFEMIT was formed. I was elected as General Secretary and David Gitari became the Chairman of the Committee. David Bussau, the Treasurer of PIM Asia, was asked to be INFEMIT's Treasurer. The INFEMIT committee consisted of Rene Padilla, Peter Savage and Tito Paredes from FTL; Vinay Samuel, David Bussau and Jonathan Chao from PIM Asia; and David Gitari, Kwame Bediako and Phineas Dube from Africa with Ron Sider and Orlando Costas from the USA. The African Theological Fellowship, the Africa regional group, was formed at this conference. It was also agreed that PIM Asia would organise and resource the first theological consultation in 1982. The decision was taken at the Bangkok Conference on Christology to set up an institution to train non-Western scholars to obtain postgraduate degrees from a reputed university.

Those present at the meeting at Five Mile Drive, Oxford were David Bussau, David Cook, Kwame Bediako, Gillian Bediako, Vinay Samuel, Chris Sugden and Mrs Hare. Barry White and Kenneth Wilson were invited but unable to be present. I chaired the meeting. I am not sure whether Ron Sider was present. Ron and I were working on several projects from 1978. These were joint projects of PIM Asia and the Ethics and Society Unit of the World Evangelical Fellowship (later 'Alliance'). Ron and I had launched the journal, *Transformation* in 1978 and Chris was also part of the team. David Cook was appointed as the Dean and Chris Sugden as the Registrar.

David, Chris and I then set out to work on the project. The original founding team was David Cook who worked on the accreditation/affiliation issues, David Bussau who managed the finances, Chris Sugden who worked on finding space where we could start, and on building relations with local churches and institutions. I coordinated the efforts, raised the needed financial support and acted as executive officer of the project.

I do not recall presenting a final plan to the INFEMIT committee as funding their travel would have cost a lot. I assumed their support and went ahead, registered the company and launched the programme in 1984. We began with a postgraduate certificate programme of Oxford University in collaboration with Wycliffe Hall (in 1984) with a few non-Western students. We also had a few PhD students registered through Westminster College, Oxford. There was no Governing Board. For the first five years, we saw ourselves as a programme of INFEMIT and reported to the INFEMIT committee when they met during the consultations that were organised. This would be once in two years, on average.

In the first few years Chris, David Cook, David Bussau and I functioned as a managing committee and built up a board after I was asked to move to Oxford in 1992 to oversee the work directly. Before then, I would travel to Oxford six times a year and spend up to three weeks each time overseeing the work directly. In 1985, INFEMIT launched the global programme called the Oxford Study on Christian Faith and Economics. This enabled the INFEMIT committee to meet in Oxford in 1986, 1987 and 1989. Major decisions were made at the INFEMIT committee meeting in Osijek, Yugoslavia in 1991 during the Osijek Consultation.

I see INFEMIT as the promoter of OCMS. The founding institution of OCMS was PIM Asia as it took responsibility for the finances of OCMS. PIM Asia's office was in Sydney, Australia where David Bussau was based. The founding team was Chris Sugden, Vinay Samuel and David Bussau. David Cook was part of it for the first three years as Dean. Chris, David Bussau and I continued for more than two decades. If we include the INFEMIT committee as founders (in my view they were not) many more would qualify as OCMS' founder members. Some of these would be: David Gitari (Chairman for the first nine years), Rene Padilla, Kwame Bediako, Ron Sider, Orlando Costas, Tito Paredes, Peter Savage, Jonathan Chao (founder of the China Graduate School of Theology, Hong Kong), Wilson Chow (China Graduate School of Theology), and Wayan Mastra (from Bali, who attended INFEMIT meetings in Oxford in the 1980s).

Funding

My role was to identify those fellow vision sharers and fellow travellers who commanded resources. They saw me as someone who could make things happen. We needed people who had resources to provide their financial support. From the beginning, two individuals from Germany were the most important supporters and provided substantial funds. Oberkirchenrat Walter Arnold, the Mission Secretary of the Evangelical Lutheran Church of Wurttemberg, was the first to understand the vision for OCMS and offer support. He introduced me to the Executive Secretary of Evangelisches Missionswerk (EMW) in Hamburg, Martin Lehmann-Habeck. Martin became an enthusiastic supporter.

Sixty per cent of OCMS' funding during this period came from Germany, thirty per cent from the USA and less than ten per cent from the UK. The only question was – do they share OCMS' vision and are they travelling in the same direction? Of German funds, sixty per cent of EMW's income came from Walter Arnold of Wurttemberg, and sixty-five per cent of the World Council of Churches' budget came from Germany. Drs Arnold and Lehmann-Habeck had discovered evangelicals who would share the gospel like them. They were not ideological liberals who did not believe the Bible. Their mission theology was also different from the evangelical mission theology of North America, which focused on church planting with little concern for society.

Other agencies positively resisted the founding of OCMS in 1983. The centre of mission society education at this time was the Selly Oak Colleges, a coalition of mission training colleges. A leader there indicated very clearly that OCMS had no right to exist, since any research in mission should be based with them. This negative reaction needed to be countered. Martin Lehmann-Habeck approached Martin Conway, a tutor at Ripon College Cuddesdon, Oxford from 1983 to 1986 and then the President of the Selly Oak Colleges, who was to become a close friend of our work and whom I met through my involvement with the Evangelism Department of the World Council of Churches. Martin dismissed the fears of Selly Oak and recommended support of this new venture. This freed up EMW to provide significant support, which has continued to this day. EMW supported the second phase of the development of the OCMS building in 1994 with £75,000 (worth £190,800 in 2023). Within twenty years, Selly Oak Colleges were dissolved.

OCMS deliberately chose not to seek permission to start up. It developed its own network of donors. It broke the mould in terms of the usual British approach to establishing a board of a Christian organisation. After twenty years, it appointed to the Board those willing to invest in its work and encouraged other Board members to be investors. OCMS sought partnership with the academy and academics rather than with mission agencies. OCMS brought non-Western mission academics to draw on the resources of Western research institutions and found encouragement from Western research and mission scholars. The first Western mission organisation to provide support was Tearfund UK, which was later joined by the Church Mission Society under the leadership of Simon Barrington-Ward. Bible Churchmen's Missionary Society (as Crosslinks was then known) paid Chris's salary for six months on his return from India. The Methodist Missionary Society gave regular support through Gordon Shaw, its General Secretary. Gordon had led my father to Christ and retained a deep affection for me. 'The Methodists should support you as you are our Methodist boy,' said Gordon who also provided for Methodist students at OCMS. It was also always a great help to know that supporting in the background was David Bussau, who had gathered funds for PIM Asia.

Supporters

The personal support of several people was important. Howard and Roberta Ahmanson of Fieldstead and Company in California had been associated with INFEMIT from its beginnings in the 1980s. Howard was concerned that so-called 'progressive left' thinking was influencing the theology espoused and developed by INFEMIT. He was keen that a conservative economic thinking be made available to the INFEMIT network as it was involved in development theology and practice. Relationships developed with Fieldstead to our mutual understanding and benefit. Fieldstead later became a substantial supporter of OCMS, and their Programme Director, Steve Ferguson, attended OCMS Board meetings.

Another generous and thoughtful friend was Phil Lundman from the United States, a friend of David Bussau, who introduced him to us. He was a member of the Assemblies of God and later joined the Roman Catholic Church. As a businessman, he devoted much of his profit to mission support. He became a generous supporter of OCMS, especially with scholarships for those from countries where Christians faced hostility and persecution, and served on the Board. Through OCMS, he met the distinguished African scholar Professor Lamin Sanneh and became a faithful supporter of him and his work. Howard, Roberta and Phil supported OCMS through their own personal family foundations.

We must not forget the late Mee-Yan Judge from Hong Kong who provided not only financial assistance but also, through her family, continues to help in many ways. Her specialty was organisational development. While Vinay did not follow all of her managerial principles, and gave a biblical justification for doing so, he always checked any new initiatives with her first, and her contribution was very significant in this field. Monty and Rosemary Barker and Mark Birchall (the Chairman of Maxco and a friend of John Stott) supported us. Mark was Chair of OCMS Board when Chris became Executive Director in 2000. He brought in Monty and Rosemary from Bristol.

St Philip and St James Church

In June 1983, I asked Chris Sugden to travel through Oxford from India en route to the conference at Wheaton, Illinois on 'The Church in Response to Human Need.' I asked him to find a redundant church that could be a possible location for OCMS. I had been inspired by the work that Patrick Sookhdeo had done at St Andrew's, Plaistow in making a large Victorian church into a worship centre and offices. Chris stayed with the Rector of St Ebbe's, the church that he had attended as a student. By that time, Keith Weston was the Rural Dean of Oxford. Chris asked Keith Weston what might be available. He replied to the effect that the question was very timely because there was a real problem for the Oxford Deanery – what to do with St Philip and St James Church in the Woodstock Road. This church had been the flagship of the Oxford Movement, opened in 1862. With the amalgamation of the parishes of St Giles, St Margaret's, and St Philip and St James in 1982, one of the three churches had to be declared redundant. Though better known, it had been decided to dispose of 'Phil and Jim.' This was perhaps because it was dark inside and very cold in the winter.

Keith Weston spelt out the problem: the Roman Catholics did not want it (as a possible cathedral), because if any church was to be a cathedral for them it would be St Aloysius in St Giles; the Simon Community (for the homeless) had expressed interest in it as a night shelter, but the north Oxford community had raised objections. The Muslims found it unacceptable because the stained glass representations of the fourteen Stations of the Cross could not be removed. St Anthony's College next door had reviewed the possibility but thought that the long-term upkeep would be too expensive. What would happen if the roof needed replacing? It had remained empty for a year, was getting overgrown and was the object of break-ins. Its windows had needed to be boarded up.

Chris Sugden visited the estate agent who was handling the disposal. He visited the church and made a formal offer of one pound for the building. We decided that the location was excellent, right in the heart of the postgraduate institutions: next door to the Latin American Study Centre, the Middle East Study Centre, the European Study Centre, the Centre for African Studies, and the Centre for the Study of African Economies. However, the consideration of the offer would take some time. In August 1983, Chris, with help from David Cook, arranged accommodation in a Westminster College room on Harcourt Hill, overlooking Oxford. However, this room had no phone facility. During the first week in the room, Chris Sugden sat at the desk and looked out on Oxford at the imposing tower of St Philip and St James, academic Oxford's most northerly spire. It was currently serving as a storage place for a collection of harmoniums, and for unrequired church furnishings. The thought came to Chris: would not the diocese prefer to have St Philip and St James occupied rather than left empty? He approached the Diocese of Oxford and suggested the following: that OCMS would rent the church from the diocese for the period while its proposal to buy it was being considered. If the proposal was turned down they would leave without prejudice. He offered £10 a year rental. The diocesan secretary, Terry Landsbert, agreed to the proposal, and dispensed with the rent. So, in the last week of September 1983, Chris moved in with tea chests that had come with his goods from India and, with an old door as a desktop, established an office in the clergy vestry. There was one power point outside in the main building for desktop lighting, and a phone line was installed.

The Arrival of Computers

In 1986, or even 1985, we were given six or ten computers as I now recall. It was before the 1987 Black Monday stock market crash when Joe Ritchie and Gary Ginter lost a lot of money. They had set up the Chicago Research and Trading Group in 1977. Joe was the major partner. We used them in the refurbished building. After the refurbishment, we received a grant from Gary for increasing the number of computers to twenty-five, which was our target. No institution at that time had so many. When the Vice-Chancellor of the University of Oxford, Ralf Dahrendorf – also the President of St Anthony's College – visited OCMS for the inauguration of its internal development, he said to me: 'Do not bother about affiliation with Oxford. It will take twenty years for the university to catch up with you. They do not understand where education is going.' He appreciated that we expected every student to be efficient in the use of computers and that distance educational studies were the future.

Chris did a bit of tidying up. He moved the harmoniums into a smaller space in the Lady Chapel. A week later, their owner had removed them altogether. It came as quite a shock, returning from India where much Christian work was done on very slender resources, suddenly to take on, willingly, six thousand square feet of redundant church building in the centre of Oxford as part of mission engagement. There was, however, a sense of stewarding a resource that had been entrusted to the OCMS team. The first question was whether this could be a long-term home. The church would require considerable modification to be useful as a study centre. It was also a Grade 1 listed building. There were doubts if consent for its modifications would be given. If not, there was no point in trying to purchase it. This was when the long process of developing plans and seeking planning permission began.

Refashioning the Building

The work on refashioning OCMS was undertaken through the good offices of OCMS' first and long-serving treasurer, David Bussau, from

Australia. David was the founder of Opportunity International, a Christian micro-finance ministry, beginning in Bali before expanding to the Philippines. In the late 70s and early 80s, David worked with me to develop the movement in India. David, himself a professional builder, persuaded good friends of his from the United States to form a working party in the summer of 1986. They cleared the path around the back of the church, and knocked through the wall from the clergy vestry to the kitchen to provide an entrance. In clearing the choir vestry, they discovered that a set of shelves used for choir music storage actually hid an original bricked up doorway. This was opened up and is now the main entrance of the centre.

The first architect we contacted at what was then The Oxford College of Advanced Technology in Headington (now Oxford Brookes University) proposed what became the final plan of the building, to make its access through the north side at the back rather than at the west door from the road. Access would therefore be through the vestry and easily controlled. The first architect was soon overwhelmed with other projects and introduced a colleague, Robert Franklin, a restoration specialist who became the Centre's architect for twenty-three years.

In close conjunction with John Ashdown, the Oxford City Conservation Officer, a set of comprehensive plans was drawn up. This involved removing the pews and the organ. The late Brian Brindley took the pews to All Saints Reading. Brian, described as a colourful Church of England clergyman, also took the stone altar from the Lady Chapel and the reserved sacrament. The organ was sold by the diocese to Headington Church, where C.S. Lewis had worshipped. The plans also involved bringing the organ loft into use and converting the choir vestry into a kitchen/refectory.

Chris Sugden and Revd Bernard Brown, the Diocesan Redundant Churches Officer, went to London to meet the Church Commissioners' Architectural Committee. The plans were presented. The chief architectural adviser was profuse with her apologies. OCMS had put a great effort into developing these plans but would have to be disappointed because even if the Church Commissioners approved them, the City Planning Department would never approve. Chris Sugden was delighted to be able to inform the committee that the plans had been drawn up with the advice and, in the case of the main seminar room at the west end, at the specific suggestion of the City Conservation Officer. The plans were approved and OCMS could move forward with a formal proposal. By 1986, the Diocese Advisory Committee (DAC) met to discuss the proposal. On the day the committee was due to meet, an article appeared in the Oxford Times indicating that the diocese was considering plans for the famous church of St Philip and St James: plans put forward by a group to use the church as a museum for ecclesiastical vestments. This was clearly a spoiling tactic.

Late in the afternoon of that day, a member of the DAC, John Gawne-Cain, the vicar of St Margaret's with St Philip and St James, informed Chris that the DAC had decided to offer the church to OCMS, by one vote, and that he had voted for the OCMS proposal. The price had increased to £20,000 (equivalent to £86,000 in 2023), which could be paid in three instalments with a five per cent mortgage. The Bishop of Oxford, Patrick Rodger, was very embarrassed and later said to me: 'It should have been given to you for one pound.' Could OCMS afford this? Advice given to us was that since most of the land in central Oxford was owned by the city and the university, this was a once-in-a-century opportunity that should not be missed.

Stephen Neill, a friend of mine from India and Cambridge and a renowned historian of mission history, suggested a funding letter. He was delighted that Oxford would have a place where Christian mission would be central and kept alive. This was sent out, signed by the former Archbishop of York, Stuart Blanch, a friend of Chris Sugden; Stephen Neill; and Alan Neech, former General Secretary of Crosslinks, the missionary society Chris had worked with in India. Neech was also a close friend of Joe Mullins, having served together in the Second World War; Joe was my senior colleague at St John's Church, Bangalore.

The letter met with many rejections and good wishes but one letter came from the Neville Russell Trust, which specialised in helping new ventures, with the promise of £12,000. Glyn Macaulay, a director who was also a close colleague of John Stott and founding Treasurer of the Langham Foundation, supported this venture and continued funding the Centre long after retiring from Neville Russell, through the Precision Trust. Confirmation had come and OCMS was able to put down the first payment of £10,000. Thus, by the end of 1986, OCMS had an office, a refectory area, and cloakrooms in what had been the flower arrangers' area at the back of the choir vestry.

The next major stage in the development of the building took place in 1994 with the conversion of the nave area into a library and study facility. The requirement of the plans was that the whole modification could be reversible so that if ever the Centre left the building, it could be restored to its original state. The plan was to undertake the modification in three phases: the central library and study carrels, the seminar room, and the organ loft. The plans were put out to tender. One firm's tender came in thirty per cent lower price than anyone else's. The requirement was that the whole project be completed in one phase. The reason was that the firm, Alfred Groves, was facing bankruptcy at the time of the building slump and would have to close after more than three hundred years of trading. They even offered to replace the Japanese oak that had been specified for the wooden construction with English oak. The underfloor heating was put in by laying a plastic sheet over the Victorian piazza-style tiling, laying plastic heating pipes on top and covering the whole in six inches of concrete. The heating did not heat the air, but people's bodies up to a height of seven feet. So, no attempt was made to heat the high open space of the 60-foot high roof. The heating of the nave was transformed. No one has ever been cold in OCMS when this heating has been working.

The final stage of the building conversion for OCMS use took place in 1994 and is commemorated by a brass plaque recording the donors. The Vice-Chancellor of CNAA attended the commissioning of the OCMS building in 1994 and affirmed the place of a Centre for Mission Studies in the work of the Open University. Regrettably, some of his successors in the academic management of the OU have not seen it that way.

Many Bricks Contributed to Building up OCMS

Many people contributed in different ways to establishing OCMS. They are otherwise unknown in the story of OCMS but without them nothing would have developed as it did.

John Gawne-Caine, the vicar of the united parishes of St Margaret's and St Giles in which St Philip and St James stood, allowed us to use St Margaret's Vicarage. The vicarage was 'redundant' and empty since Bishop Colin Winter had lived there in exile from South Africa. This gave me a place to stay when visiting Oxford. In 1984, Bishop Michael Nazir Ali, Bishop of Raiwind in Pakistan, had to flee because of death threats to his family. Archbishop Robert Runcie of Canterbury invited them to England and appointed him as the study coordinator for the 1988 Lambeth Conference (at which he invited Chris and me to attend as 'journalists' and from which we wrote 'Lambeth – a View from the Two Thirds World' (SPCK 1989)) and learnt how Lambeth Conferences operated. St Margaret's Vicarage was in place to provide somewhere for him and his family to stay. It also had a flat where visitors and INFEMIT scholars who came to teach at OCMS could stay.

Carole Anderson, seconded to us and supported by Gary Ginter, worked with us for three years to build up our computer expertise. Neil Mawhinney managed our administration for nearly a decade. He was paid from PIM Asia funds, who also covered my salary and the half salary of £16,000 a year we paid to Michael Nazir Ali for three years and provided housing. The housing costs were met by OCMS.

OCMS' own needs did not require the use of the whole building. The organ loft was let out to two newly established organisations: Quality and Equality, and SIMA UK. Quality and Equality was founded by Mee-Yan Judge. Mee-Yan has been a major supporter, counsellor to and investor in OCMS. She devised a series of management seminars on Christian leadership which were offered to OCMS and wider Christian community in 2004. From these, Mee-Yan was requested to do major consultancies for the International Fellowship of Evangelical Students and other Christian organisations worldwide. Chris Sugden, as a participant in a Christian summer camp, had known Nick Isbister, the founder of SIMA UK. SIMA specialised in giving career consultancy and headhunting for Christian organisations. Andrew Wingfield-Digby, the founder of Christians in Sport, came to see whether OCMS would have suitable facilities for his fledgling organisation. Mee-Yan Judge's advice that OCMS should bring the whole building into use meant that Quality and Equality and SIMA eventually found new facilities for their own expanding work. For some time, the OCMS building was an incubator for these two organisations that were, like OCMS, starting out.

CONCLUSION

The establishment of OCMS confirmed that mission studies can be pursued in a British university context by practicing Christian leaders from the non-Western world who did not have to mask their faith, and had the freedom to engage in topics that a university department considered as proper subjects for research. They could see their faith, work and mission concerns as worthy of extensive and intensive research engagement. It confirmed that mission studies and research were global enterprises and particularly important for the growing churches of the non-Western world.

OCMS was a research institution in the heart of a prestigious Western university run by a network of Christian leaders from countries in the periphery of power, and from once colonial nations. This signalled that the churches in the majority world were ready to appropriate the best of Western scholarship in developing their own approaches, strategies and theologies of engaging with the world. It also meant that they would make their contribution to the global church not just with church growth but also in the areas of mission theologies and public theologies. Particularly important was the impact on OCMS students from non-Western contexts who came to an institution owned and run by non-Western Christian leaders. They were not guests but family, and this sense of OCMS as a global Christian family became a precious gift to students.

CHAPTER 2

CREATIVITY, EXPERIMENTATION AND NEW WAYS OF DOING THEOLOGY

VINAY SAMUEL AND CHRISTOPHER SUGDEN

On reading Kissinger's book on Bismarck, *The White Revolutionaries* Vinay found a way of describing what we did with the formation of the International Fellowship of Evangelical Mission Theologians (INFEMIT).[1] An international order of evangelicalism developed from the Western missionary movements of the nineteenth and twentieth centuries with the formation of international networks of mission societies: the World Evangelical Alliance, the Billy Graham Association and the Lausanne Committee. Post-Lausanne in 1974, it was clear to some in the non-Western world that this order entrenched the power of Western evangelicals, promoted and established their theologies, established institutions in the non-Western world that they controlled and enabled them to shape and control evangelicalism globally. The rapid growth of evangelical faith in the non-Western world, particularly in Latin America and Africa, and the emergence of Western-trained, non-Western leaders and scholars, produced a conflict of ideas that came to the fore in the 1974 Lausanne Conference. The resulting declaration at least incorporated the ideas and views of mission from the non-Western world, which were set out in the radical discipleship statement.[2]

A push back started soon after Lausanne to reverse the emerging understanding of mission that Lausanne had accepted. This came to a head in the Consultation on World Evangelisation (COWE at

[1] Now the International Fellowship of Mission as Transformation.
[2] This can be seen in *Radical Discipleship* by Chris Sugden, Marshalls, 1981.

Pattaya (Thailand) in 1980. Some of us from the non-Western world recognised that the way to change the existing international order of evangelicalism was to remain within its superstructure to affirm our identity as evangelicals but work to dismantle its existing Western hegemony. We did this by forming our own international networks, building our own training and research institutions, developing leaders, and ensuring that we did the academic work to back our understanding of mission, particularly mission as transformation.

In time, we knew that this would reshape evangelicalism. INFEMIT, the international network, and its institution, the Oxford Centre for Mission Studies (OCMS), were products of that strategy. We did not set up alternatives to the existing international networks such as the World Evangelical Fellowship (WEF) and the Lausanne Committee for World Evangelisation (LCWE). We formed a network that worked with and within both of them and with the World Council of Churches (WCC). In the 1990s, INFEMIT members were part of the Strategy and Theological Commissions of LCWE, members of the Theological Commission of WEF, and members of the Commission on World Mission and Evangelisation (CWME) of the WCC. We were confident that in time they would change. History will be the judge of this strategy.

Early Years

A Decolonised Institution

Our object was to create a decolonised institution in the heart of Western academia. We related to the academy on our terms. We were creating space to pioneer an emerging way of doing research, which reflected the new post-colonial reality in the academic centres of the Western world. This new way of doing research had four dimensions: epistemology, research methodology, studying history from below, and reflective practice.

Epistemology has to do with knowing, identifying, gathering, organising and interpreting knowledge. How does that relate to the conviction that the gospel of Jesus is the truth about the world and all that is in it? This raises the question: where does truth lie? Does it lie in a rational argument or in experience? The Western academy believes that knowledge is the key to liberation. Our approach privileged the truth, as it is in Jesus; this also investigated how to understand, explain and apply truth. In what form, therefore, does truth come?

All experience has a spiritual dimension; therefore story, narrative, testimony, intuition, sensibilities and traditions of learning (such as proverbs) were all important in accessing truth. We believed that research theses at OCMS at the time came under all these categories. The spiritual dimension was especially attractive to researchers from Pentecostal churches, a number of whom enrolled with OCMS. Our researchers and the way we approached knowledge and truth attracted some of the best academics in the fields of anthropology, history and sociology who were willing to supervise our researchers. Though they were part of the Western academy and its traditions, they were willing to explore these dimensions and many gave their time free of charge. Some of those who examined the work of our students were impressed by the new knowledge that such approaches produced in, for example, the new way of understanding history from below.

A key theme of our research methodology was reflective practice. OCMS owes a large debt of gratitude to Bernard Farr who worked with us from Westminster College and eventually joined our team. Together with Farr, we developed the MTh in Applied Theology of Oxford University at Westminster College. OCMS was able to enhance the programme by adding a number of developments to it, such as the six-week residential research seminar at OCMS with two senior advisers, Lamin Sanneh, the Professor of Missions and Christianity at Yale University, and M.M. Thomas of the Christian Institute for the Study of Religion and Society (CISRS) in Bangalore, India. This demonstrated the capacity of non-Western students to do studies at a postgraduate level that was acceptable to Oxford

University. Sanneh described a PhD done at OCMS on two Asian mission theologians as 'a dynamic impetus of a global theological current. The literature on contextual theology and situational ethics now has a standard to rise to.'[3]

The third dimension was to look at history from below. These were not indigenous histories but histories of Christian action and growth looked at from below and privileging the way of understanding the history of people in the communities involved. If people experienced miraculous events, these were not squeezed out of the story or put into the straitjacket of rationality. Churches in India, Africa and Latin America told their own stories of how they related their understanding of the Christian faith to their context and culture and negotiated the issues raised. What did they adopt from the Christian faith and why? What did they retain from their own culture and why? This produced records of how indigenous Christianity responded to the gospel of Jesus as truth. The main protagonists and actors were indigenous Christians and community leaders, not a church planting movement or missionary planted churches, which privileged the missionary enterprise with the understandable motives of demonstrating the impact of missionaries and securing further support.

The fourth dimension of the decolonised approach to research was the transforming power of the gospel. Our research programme was mission minded. We were not shy of believing that the gospel did transform people's lives, communities and nations. These impact studies were not set aside as an area that could not be researched. Such transformational studies asked what change did the power of the gospel bring. Five themes can be discerned in these years of consolidation and experimentation:

[3] See this quote on the back cover of Chris Sugden, *Seeking the Asian Face of Jesus – the Practice and Theology of Christian Social Witness in India 1974–1996*, Regnum, 1997.

1. Institutional partnerships with institutions of the academy.
2. Development of supervisors.
3. 'Beginning Research' seminar aimed at preparing people to develop research skills before they start their research.
4. Deciding how to make the best use of the six-week to three-month period that the students spend in residence. For this, we developed a weekly research seminar where, during their residence, students presented a chapter from their current state of work to fellow students and academic staff for engagement and critique.
5. Summer schools which positioned OCMS globally and brought the world to OCMS. The topics were to develop contextual wholistic theology in a number of current themes. The presentations and reports of the summer schools were published in the journal *Transformation*.

Institutional Partnerships

In the beginning, institutional partnerships helped us to launch OCMS. It was important to seek accreditation from our university partners, and not affiliation to be absorbed into them.

The first of these was Westminster College, Oxford, a Methodist foundation. Dr David Cook was on the Westminster staff after his time at St John's College Nottingham where Chris Sugden got to know him when training there. Vinay Samuel had met him at the Ethics Conference at High Leigh in 1978. He had shared the way in which the Council of National Academic Awards (CNAA) facilitated distance learning for postgraduate degrees at Westminster College. Vinay invited Cook to come to India in 1981 to advise the Association for Theological Education by Extension (TAFTEE) on developing its postgraduate studies. From this, Vinay decided to invite Cook to share this postgraduate distance learning process at the consultation on Sharing Jesus in the Two Thirds World in 1982. Cook introduced us to the Principal, Revd Dr

Kenneth Wilson (later OBE) who was also a council member of the CNAA. The first OCMS PhD students, of which Chris was one,[4] were registered with the CNAA through Westminster which allowed OCMS to use its framework. The college gave OCMS its first office space in the college before it purchased St Philip and St James Church.

A second institution was Wycliffe Hall Oxford, an Anglican theological college that was a five-minute walk from St Philip and St James Church. Its Principal was Canon Dr Richard (Dick) France, a noted New Testament scholar and former theological educator in Nigeria. France being at Wycliffe connected us with the one-year postgraduate course, which we thought was essential for our students to get the necessary background in foundation biblical studies, theology, history, theological methodologies, and as an introduction to writing essays and research papers. Most of our students would not have had the preparation for research studies that British university courses provide. The first steps in this direction were to enter candidates for the Oxford University Certificate in Theology, with a specialism in Development Studies and in Communication Studies. Richard and his successor as Principal, Revd Dr Alister McGrath, were especially helpful. Candidates were enrolled with Wycliffe Hall, attended their lectures and took the university examinations. The certificate allowed a degree of candidate choice in papers and candidates were able to present essays focusing on their specialty. Residence was required for approximately six months a year over two years. Candidates from the Philippines, New Zealand and Mexico were successful in gaining awards. Some others failed to complete their requirements. Our connection with Wycliffe Hall and their postgraduate certificate course enabled us to be recognised as a postgraduate institution based in the city of Oxford and recognition as ocms.ac.uk; it also enabled us to make use of the university libraries and Regents Park

[4] Regnum Books published his thesis; see Sugden, *Seeking the Asian Face*, 1997. The bibliography contains lists of the writings of Vinay up to this period.

College library which specialised in mission history. Our experience with the certificate course helped us in designing the 'Beginning Research' seminar.[5] Eventually, in 1996, Wycliffe Hall became a permanent private hall of Oxford University, which meant they were unable to continue to enter candidates for the university certificate. OCMS applied for the ability to enter candidates on its own but a review conducted by the university found we lacked the recognised faculty.

A third institution was Regents Park College, a Baptist theological college, twelve minutes' walk from OCMS. The Principal, Dr Barry White, a fine evangelical and proud of his connections with the Baptist Missionary Society, was also Chair of the Oxford Theology Faculty and was keen to integrate OCMS as much as possible into the university.

All three Principals recognised and strongly supported the OCMS vision of developing the training of theologians and church leaders from the Global South. In partnership with these colleges, OCMS was able to present candidates for doctoral and MPhil degrees with the CNAA, and the Oxford Postgraduate Certificate in Theology with Wycliffe Hall and Regents Park College. These connections with Westminster College, Wycliffe Hall and Regents Park College helped to establish OCMS as a recognised theological institution and part of the Oxford scene in double quick time with hardly any students or staff.

In time, the CNAA merged with the Open University (OU) and OCMS degrees became OU degrees. As OCMS numbers grew, the OU set a limit of fifteen students and so partnerships were developed with the University of Leeds through Dr Haddon Willmer, whom Chris had known when he was a curate in Leeds, and with the University of Wales through Dr D.P. Davies. At one point, OCMS was in partnership with three universities. Each university brought its own specialty. The Theology Department at

[5] See the section on research seminars below.

Leeds had a focus on biblical studies through Haddon Willmer. The Open University was not able to help in this area, as it had no theology or religion faculty as such.

Such partnerships always depended on a champion within the institution. The development of OCMS was marked, therefore, by friendships with leaders in theological training institutions rather than solely by the interests of the institutions themselves. Such has been the way of Christian ministry and mission since Jesus chose twelve people who were friends, relations and work colleagues of each other to form the first nucleus of his movement.

Why did the universities accept our students in partnership? Our champions were excited with the vision of OCMS and the access that OCMS gave them to mature Christian leaders who had a passion for mission and ministry as the context of their study, and proved to be of good quality. We could not make much progress with Oxford University in spite of the fact that we enrolled Christian leaders in their Certificate in Theology. Oxford did not countenance distance learning at that time. Once OCMS started its MA programmes, we no longer enrolled students in the Oxford Certificate course.

University Partnerships

The vision of OCMS was to provide access to a university system in the Western world through which Christian leaders, especially from Africa, Asia and Latin America, could undertake research degrees up to doctorate level while resident for the most part in their own countries.

Stewart Weir, the administrator of the CNAA, carried out the first validation in 1986. He visited the Centre, and assessed the access it had to libraries in Oxford and academics. He judged that it was capable of providing the appropriate environment, support and resources to enable people to register and complete PhD programmes under the CNAA.

The CNAA also validated the polytechnics in the United Kingdom. The polytechnics wanted to become universities and the

Conservative government wanted to increase the number of university places. Kenneth Clark, the Education Secretary, therefore proposed to give all polytechnics charters. It was pointed out to him that the CNAA also validated the degrees of a further eighty institutions. He recommended that they should affiliate with their local universities. OCMS joined with these institutions to meet with officials of the Department of Education to advise them that had the local universities in question been adequate to meet their academic needs, they would not have gone to the trouble of seeking separate registration with the CNAA. These institutions were also very aware that their local university could give initial recognition but then absorb the institution, and its assets, totally into its structure. To anticipate the next stages of the story, this is exactly what happened to the institutions that joined the Open University.

However, at this stage, the proposal was made by OCMS as well as by others that the CNAA seek recognition by the Open University, given that both were devoted to extending the frontiers of university education to non-residential studies. While this proposal was being considered OCMS, with other institutions, framed plans for establishing a new university altogether to embrace these eighty institutions. Further meetings took place with the Department of Education which led to the CNAA, with its entire staff and its building near King's Cross, being taken into the Open University as the Centre for Validation Services.

The British system of validating courses and programmes was most suitable for OCMS. Other countries validate institutions by looking at buildings, libraries and faculty members. The CNAA and the Open University looked at the programme. This partnership went well for a number of years. Then, a new culture came into university education. Gone forever were the days when Stewart Weir could come and assess OCMS in half a day. After five years, the Open University conducted a validation visit on OCMS. They judged that because certain paper trails were not in place, OCMS' validation needed to be suspended until the administration caught up with the throughput of work. Simon Lumby was recruited from St John's College Nottingham in 1995 where he had been Academic Administrator, and introduced the necessary paper trails of reports and records. This proved valuable in the long term, but disadvantaged a number of students whose work could not be registered or advanced while the suspension was in place.

While all this was going on, Korean students at OCMS foresaw a problem. The Open University had no geographical location as such. They were concerned that their degree would not secure sufficient recognition in Korea. This was at the point when OCMS had yet to establish its brand through its graduates. At this time, exploration was taking place of universities that might validate master's degrees at OCMS. The University of Wales was among them. D.P. Davies, (DP) was the head of the Department of Theology and the Pro Vice-Chancellor of the University of Wales. He was a friend of Bernard Farr. A minibus went down to Cardiff to meet with DP, to explore the possibility of securing validation for doctoral degrees with them. Vinay Samuel, David Samuel and Chris were in the party. A formal proposal was made; a team from the University of Wales came to visit and awarded OCMS their validation. For its part, OCMS would have to recruit ten students a year in order for the research programme to pay the consolidated validation fee. At the first five-year evaluation, the University of Wales invited OCMS to accept a formal relationship as an affiliated institution of the University of Wales. It was pointed out that such an invitation was rare after only the first five-year evaluation. This was at their invitation, not our request. We were now sufficiently recognised as having our own identity and contribution that we did not fear absorption.

It proved great wisdom to have two validations since eventually, the Open University incorporated the research institutions of the former CNAA and determined to centralise all research in its own research departments. OCMS pointed out that the Open University had no theology research department and that this decision reversed undertakings that had been made to OCMS; but to no avail.

In academic administration, it really does matter if a Pharaoh arises who knew not Joseph. This is what happened with the University of Leeds. In developing its master's programmes (of which more below), OCMS held a week-long conference in June 1996 to investigate the worldwide need for postgraduate mission studies for itself and other institutions. A number of British universities attended to present their opportunities to overseas institutions who were attending. At that conference, the proposal offered by the University of Leeds was most attractive. The then Head of the Department of Theology at Leeds, Haddon Willmer, supported it. Leeds validated OCMS' first MA courses (of which more below). Haddon suggested that it might be advantageous for some OCMS students to register as PhD students with the University of Leeds because, with a dedicated Theology Department, they could provide supervision – especially in African Studies. This was agreed. On his retirement as Head of Department, Haddon became a part-time research tutor at OCMS and contributed greatly to the supervision of students under all three university validations.

Changes of staff at Leeds who did not share the enthusiasm of their predecessors and growing concerns that government regulations would rule out the validation of programmes at institutions which OCMS partnered in other countries meant that the regime of validation became so restrictive as to prove impossible. First the master's registration and then the research registration were discontinued.

CNAA, OU, Wales and Leeds: to this list must be added the University of Leiden in Holland. Through Jan Jongeneel, it was possible to register students for whom even the six weeks' residence in the UK was impossible to fulfil, and also who would benefit from writing their thesis in French, their first language. David

Koudougeret of the Bible Society of the Central African Republic completed his OCMS doctorate under their auspices in 2000.

The University of Oxford must also be added to this list. Almost from its inception, there were those who wanted to benefit from OCMS' focus on study in wholistic mission practice but who clearly did not need and were probably not up to doctoral studies. Parallel with these developments, OCMS was encouraged by Keith Ward, the Regius Professor of Divinity at Oxford, to propose a joint programme with the university for a master's degree in World Christianity. A curriculum was developed and OCMS faculty identified to contribute particular modules. The university then indicated that it did not have the faculty to provide the modules it was responsible to deliver. The programme remained at the proposal stage.

These two developments with the University of Oxford built on a range of informal engagements. From 1985, OCMS taught the mission courses for the Certificate in Theology for Mansfield College and for Wycliffe Hall. Its Tuesday lectures began as a series of lectures for these courses. OCMS contributed to the African Studies seminars, and it trained and encouraged the first steps of researchers who then secured university scholarships for their own doctorate programmes or who developed global careers and now head Oxford University programmes.

Supervisors

A key issue in these early years was to identify supervisors from scholars in the UK for our doctoral students. While the universities provided the framework and the process for doctoral research, they themselves were unable to provide supervisors. To develop the research dimension, OCMS built a network of research supervisors who shared its vision, and most of whom contributed their time on a voluntary basis. These were established academics (not OCMS faculty). They gave their time freely for the love of training non-Western students. They negotiated any possible conflict of interest with their employing institution very well. They included Professor Andrew Walls at the Universities of Aberdeen and Edinburgh; Professor Terry Ranger, Head of the Africa Studies Centre from Oxford University; Professor Deryke Belshaw, East Anglia, Development Studies; and, as mentioned earlier, Haddon Willmer of Leeds. Some of them were distinguished leaders in their fields and recently retired academics. Due to their generosity of spirit, the validating universities often provided 'sleeping' supervisors to give notional oversight while OCMS recruited the main supervisors who gave of their expertise willingly for often no more than a notional honorarium. These key friends, with others, became part of OCMS. Thus, OCMS was much more than a recruiting sergeant for the universities. After ten years, OCMS had fifty-six supervisors in the UK guiding our research scholars. Again, many of these supervisors were good friends of the founding Board members. For example, Andrew Walls was the supervisor of Revd Dr Kwame Bediako from Ghana. In this way, OCMS was able to grow without having a large staff and faculty.

Research Seminars

A major problem was that whereas Western students had had three years' preparation for their research degree in the UK academic culture, those from Africa, Asia and Latin America found themselves plunged into the deep end. Therefore, they spent a great deal of time working out what they were supposed to do in their research programme. The universities themselves gave very little guidance. Starting in 1986, OCMS and the Langham Scholarship Programme led by John Stott together pioneered a two-day seminar at the beginning of the academic year in September for those coming from overseas to begin a UK PhD programme. The first seminar was held in what is now the kitchen of OCMS. Presentations were made on both the academic and spiritual dimensions of beginning research. London Bible College, Whitefield Institute and Tyndale House formed part of the team for shorter or longer periods. These seminars were held each year for a forty-eight-hour period. The year 2007 was the first year in which John Stott did not himself give a presentation. Over this period, other institutions such as the London School of Theology instituted their own introductory programmes.

Terry Ranger, Director of African Studies housed in St Anthony's College, next door to OCMS, suggested a joint seminar with OCMS in the academic year 1991–1992 on themes of mission. Researchers from OCMS and the university alternated weekly seminar presentations based on their research for the OCMS and university's postgraduate community. This particular seminar was so much appreciated in OCMS that it became a regular Wednesday morning seminar at which OCMS researchers presented the latest in their research for discussion by their peers and faculty. Supervisors of students attended when their student was presenting. These seminars were a key feature in the six-week residence that students put in every year at Oxford. In this way, Oxford University faculty attended the seminar and were very complimentary about the range of global expertise available for students to engage with.

Terry and his wife Shelagh Ranger had experience in Zimbabwe and became supportive of our Zimbabwean students. It was the time when many were seeking refuge from the Mugabe regime. Shelagh was very much involved in Refugee Welcome. OCMS held a summer school on refugees. We also welcomed refugees from the military regime in Burma/Myanmar. Through Terry and St Anthony's College, OCMS was allowed to log on to the university's internet connection. Another player who was a great help was Andy Buck who looked after OCMS' technology, and continues to do so to this day. One of the Oxford students who attended these seminars was Sabina Alkire, now Professor of Poverty and Human Development at Oxford. Sabina, doing an MSc in Economics, asked Vinay what subject she should research. He suggested a study of the ethics of Amartya Sen's economics. Her MSc thesis on the topic won the George Medley graduate prize, and her doctorate, subsequently published, was on the same subject.

Another supporter of the research seminar was Haddon Willmer. He and his wife Hilary and their children spent a month in ministry at St John's Church Bangalore as part of his three-month sabbatical, which took place in Bangalore, and also visiting Partners in Mission Asia members in Malaysia and the Philippines. Chris had known Haddon (a Cambridge graduate), a member of Moortown Baptist Church and University Professor during his time in Leeds. He suggested that Haddon come to India as part of his sabbatical, and Vinay Samuel arranged for him and his family to stay in the United Theological College in Bangalore. After his first week, Haddon reviewed his experience in meeting different groups of people throughout Bangalore, both the middle-class members of St John's Church and the working poor in the slum areas where Colleen and Vinay had established a congregation. Haddon noted that, 'everywhere I went, I sensed that people expected God would naturally intervene in their lives miraculously. They just take it for granted. This has changed my whole understanding of religion and society.'

The MA Programme

Bernard Farr was asked to investigate the possibility of developing an MA programme and he suggested trying D.P. Davies, who was then the Pro Vice-Chancellor of the University of Wales and one of his friends. The MA programme was developed to explore areas of Applied Theology in Development, Communication, and HIV Aids. These courses were needed, with the development of contextual theology, to express Christian response and action to some of the pressing challenges in the Global South. The focus was not on evangelism in a vacuum, but on addressing the context and cultures in which the gospel was communicated. Context was studied through the MA in Applied Theology and Development; culture was studied through the MA in Communication which David Adams, an executive of Transworld Radio, assisted in developing. It was very important to develop these courses, as nothing was available on them in the Global

South for Christian leaders. Thus, it was that Prem James, the director of Far East Broadcasting Associates (India) came to study the MA in Communication.

The motivation for cultivating the master's courses was to introduce study and skills development to those without prior training in a Western academic context. Thus, Bishop Joshua Banda did a masters in HIV Aids prior to doing his PhD examining the effectiveness of discipleship training in reducing the incidence of HIV Aids in Zambia.

GROWTH AND DEVELOPMENT

The early years of OCMS were marked by the promotion of wholistic mission theology through publications, summer schools and identifying how to support mission activists in the Global South. This was done by enabling those from the Global South to research their own contexts with rigour and a biblically informed understanding. OCMS' main concern was to be the theological arm of INFEMIT and promote the wholistic theology of transformation, which INFEMIT had pioneered and developed. The development of wholistic theology in the international community can be traced back to the World Evangelical Fellowship (WEF) consultations on Simple Lifestyle and on Theology of Development, held at High Leigh, Hoddesdon UK in March 1980. These were sponsored by the Unit on Ethics and Society of the WEF, convened by Ron Sider with Vinay Samuel as Chair. We realised that scholars from the non-Western world were needed to engage with this and David Cook was invited to come to India in 1981. He shared with us the way in which distance learning for postgraduate degrees was facilitated by the CNAA. As a result, Vinay Samuel decided to invite him to share this at the consultation on Sharing Jesus in the Two Thirds World, in 1982.

Developments in Evangelical Theology

One of the significant traditions that developed in the evangelical movement in the twentieth century was that the text (of the Bible itself) became the very presence of the idea of God. This was in reaction to the dominance of idealism in nineteenth century thought, where the 'idea' became supreme without relation to the scripture, which was 'deconstructed' by biblical criticism into numerous historical layers and myths. In reaction, many evangelicals saw the text itself as the presence of 'the idea' (of God) and fused God and the text of the Bible. For the poets of the Romantic movement, beauty had to have a beautiful text; similarly, for the evangelicals, the Bible itself mediated the presence of God. Thus, idealism was textualised. As long as the evangelicals remained married to the text alone, they were always going to be a minority. The deconstruction of the text continued apace in theological education and thus the very presence of God was removed from the thought world of many Christian leaders. The Bible became, therefore, a witness to an ideal. We need to realise that the presence of God cannot be fully captured in a text. The Pentecostal movement broke free of this by focusing on the experience of God.

The movement for the wholistic theology of transformation focused on the interaction of the gospel with particular contexts. The backgrounds for this movement were: the alternatives of pure idealism as represented by liberal theology which refused to be directed by the text; the textualism of evangelicals who locked God up in the text of the Bible; and the Pentecostals who stressed experience. This theology was taken up by Partnership in Mission Asia following the Lausanne Conference on World Evangelisation of 1984 and, more especially, the statement of radical discipleship that was adopted by many there.

Our work on wholistic mission between 1981 and 1984 prepared for the coming of OCMS, to witness to mission and bring its gifts from India to the UK. During 1977 and 1978, we did research into urban mission in India. This was with Cynthia Stephen who researched urban issues in New Delhi, Mumbai and Bangalore. In 1978, we collaborated with ministries among the urban poor: with Bombay Urban Industrial League for Development (BUILD and Chris Wigglesworth) in Mumbai (Bombay); with Raju Abraham in

Calcutta; and with C.B. Samuel in Delhi. Vinay and Colleen began doing this by founding Divya Shanthi Community Church in Lingarajapuram, a slum in north Bangalore.

In 1983, Vinay and Chris toured the UK, especially visiting the Bible Churchmen's Missionary Society (BCMS) and to focus on the development of OCMS. BCMS had supported Chris and his wife Elaine in India and continued for their first months back in the UK at the close of their ministry there. Our visit to the UK included attending the Evangelical Coalition for Urban Mission (ECUM) conference, and our contribution to the Lausanne booklets on *Gospel and the Poor* and *Urban Ministry*. Through engagements such as these, OCMS became a global centre for promoting wholistic mission theology and transforming society through churches. The Fuller School of World Mission in Pasadena, California focused on unreached peoples with a mainly 'evangelistic' approach based on church planting. These were the two major approaches in the 1980s and were represented in the Lausanne networks.

OCMS worked closely with the World Evangelical Theological Commission and its Unit on Ethics and Society convened by Dr Ron Sider of Eastern Baptist Seminary, Philadelphia; also, with the team who produced the Church of England report, 'Faith in the City' led by Robert Haslam and Revd Pat Dearnley, Chris's predecessor at St George's Church Leeds. In this process, OCMS was working on common ground between evangelical and ecumenical networks on the ground. This was the first such exploration. It shaped 'Faith in the City' and, through that, the policy of the UK government. It also set the ball rolling on evangelical–ecumenical dialogues with the WCC and Raymond Fung (the then Secretary for Evangelism in the WCC's Commission on World Mission and Evangelism).

The question was how to promote such a theology, which was initially regarded with suspicion by many evangelical leaders in both the West and the Global South (especially where institutions and projects were dependent on North American money). Steps in the right direction were to encourage reflection on wholistic theology of mission and train others in both practice and reflection on their practice

To encourage reflection on wholistic mission practice, OCMS started a series of summer schools that took place over two or three weeks in August each year (the academic summer break in the UK academic calendar). People attending these schools returned to their places of ministry and developed their theology and practice in ministries to children, refugees, and the urban poor. They enabled people to get a taste of the process of reflection and study in Oxford, surrounded by the resources of books and journals, and to reflect together on their mission practice in the light of the Bible. These summer schools became the recruiting grounds for people to undertake postgraduate programmes at OCMS themselves or recommend it to others.

This 'spirit' of OCMS found particular expression in the nine-year study on Christian Faith and Economics. This took place in several locations around the world, including Oxford, Agra and Moscow. This study process addressed how to engage justice in the economic order to address poverty. It developed the movement for Christian microfinance, which engaged communities of the poor to develop very small-scale enterprises started by making loans available to a circle of people engaged in growing, sewing, and marketing produce for their communities. This has become a major plank in processes of community development among poor communities fostered by Western development agencies.

OCMS moved in a positive direction to discover that the gospel was wider and deeper than accepting Christ and being born again. OCMS sought to express the gospel of the Kingdom of God as it engages with life. It was not obsessed with the Global South's own decolonisation. OCMS leaders held that to discover their true identity in Christ, as Indians for example, meant discovering their own calling in Christ, not focusing on decolonisation. Their focus was to work on how to express the gospel of Christ and its transforming power in their own cultures authentically; their faithful presence in their culture as Christians; and release the power of the gospel in their culture. We were not obsessed with trying to identify the wrongs of the past that must be set right. We did not engage in identity politics to get rid of something imposed on us. We were involved in a more positive engagement to develop identities that are authentic and transformative.

To understand these developments, it helps to appreciate the Actor Network Theory, where changes and developments come from human actors, rather than movements, ideas and forces. Theologies and ideas do exist apart from human actors. Such actors may be individuals or a collective. The early apostles were such actors. What happens is that their actions become routinised into traditions that then override the role of the actors. OCMS was creating actors who could continue to engage in these fields – actors who could be more than people who gathered and used resources on projects. They could build institutions to foster ideas, ideologies and convictions. The difference between building a business and building an institution such as OCMS was that the 'products' of OCMS were people who were strengthened in their convictions that they could change society and equip others to do so: the development of actors who could build other things. For this reason, OCMS did not seek to develop into a university but rather into a training institution. It needed some degree of routinisation but also its place was to enable people to question current situations and practices.

The process of routinisation and sacralisation is a feature of religious traditions. For example, the Holy Communion/Eucharist is at the heart of the Roman Catholic Church's religious observance. For some Roman Catholics, the presence of Christ is routinised and sacralised in 'going to Mass'. Similarly, some evangelicals have routinised and sacralised the presence of Christ in the text of the Bible.

International Funding Support Based on a Shared Vision

OCMS had to address this challenge. In 1991, the Board faced the question of whether to continue its work or close. It had no regular income stream and numbers enrolling were not going well. It appeared to have no future.

Rene Padilla, the Chair of the Board, presented the challenge to Vinay Samuel that he should come to lead OCMS in person or it would have to close. Vinay put a fleece out that both money and visas for his family would be made available. The latter came quite easily. For the former, Joel Carpenter of the Pew Foundation arranged a three-year grant from the foundation that repeated over a period of nine years. Carpenter had discovered the INFEMIT network when, in the Wheaton College library, he came across the record of its first consultation, held in Bangkok in 1982, *Sharing Jesus in the Two Thirds World*.[6] He had not known that evangelicals with such a wholistic approach existed and started an attempt to get in touch. INFEMIT held a number of conferences from 1986 to 1989. Carpenter attended the INFEMIT conference in Osijek (Yugoslavia; now Croatia) along with representatives of the McLelland Foundation and Fieldstead and Co. These major evangelical foundations knew that this wholistic approach to mission, as expressed by OCMS, was the future for evangelicals.

In this way, OCMS and its leadership moved from being suspect persons in the evangelical world to being people who had a legitimate role in the future of evangelicalism. OCMS became a good investment.

Summer Schools

From the outset, OCMS sought to stimulate and encourage others rather than undertake everything itself. Its first programmes, even before any academic programmes began, were summer schools. These

[6] Vinay Samuel and Chris Sugden (eds), *Partnership in Mission Asia*, Bangalore, 1983, republished by Eerdmans, USA, 1984.

positioned OCMS globally and brought the world to OCMS. The topics were to develop contextual wholistic theology in a number of current areas.

The first summer schools were held in August 1984, eleven months after OCMS' opening. They were located in Westminster College, Oxford. They focused on the topics of Urban Mission, and Development and Transformation, which grew out of the work of INFEMIT in the years since 1980.

Under the Lausanne Committee for World Evangelisation, Ray Bakke had pioneered a series of city-wide seminars on urban mission. In 1981, Vinay Samuel invited Ray Bakke, at that time at Northern Baptist Theological Seminary in Chicago, to do training in urban mission in India. His focus was on 'Exegeting the City'. He was invited to introduce this concept to the UK and to meet those who were carrying the brief for urban mission among evangelicals. In 1983, he visited the UK and addressed the first conference of the ECUM. Others involved were Greg Smith and Michael Eastman of Frontier Youth Trust (FYT).

This summer school proved to be forward-looking. Among those attending were Michael Eastman of the FYT who would be a commissioner on the Archbishop of Canterbury's Commission, whose report in 1986 was entitled Faith in the City; and Revd Patrick Dearnley who would be the first Director of the Church Urban Fund. This group also developed relationships with Ray Bakke and visited his urban mission conventions in Chicago. They brought this concept to the UK and started the regular Jesus in the City celebrations.

The summer school on Development and Transformation followed up on the process that had culminated at the Wheaton Consultation on the Church in Response to Human Need (1983). In succeeding years, in its own building of St Philip and St James Church, OCMS tackled several other topics in the weeklong summer schools (usually held in July or August). These topics included: Fund Raising for Christian Organisations (with the Chair of World

Vision); in 1986, Base Ecclesial Communities focusing on the House Church phenomenon and its parallels with the BECs in Latin America, and the Church in China (with the late Jonathan Chao); and Engagement with Other Faiths (with Bishops Michael Nazir Ali and Kenneth Cragg). The summer school on Micro-enterprise Development (MED) (with David Bussau) played a role in profiling what was to become a highly successful Christian ministry which accounted for eighty per cent of evangelical involvement in development. The local church and global mission reflected the increasing involvement by local churches directly in mission activities, rather than through a development agency.

In winter 1987, OCMS hosted the First Oxford Conference on Christian Faith and Economics, based in the Examination Schools of Oxford University. This prepared the ground for the Second Oxford Conference in 1990, which was held at OCMS. Vinay Samuel, Ron Sider and Rene Padilla led these conferences. The second conference produced the Oxford Statement on Christian Faith and Economics, which was a significant rapprochement between left and right wing views on economics following the collapse of communism. The Third Oxford Conference was held in Agra (India) in 1994. In 1995, OCMS held a winter school on refugees with Emmanuel Kolini (later Archbishop of Rwanda) and Alan Nichols.[7] Part of this included a major session on the genocide in Rwanda with Tharcisse Gatwa.[8] In 1995, the winter school took the theme 'Disability' and in 1996, 'Children in Need' in partnership with the Viva organisation.

In 2003, OCMS held a summer school on the churches' response to HIV/Aids. This highlighted the MA programme in HIV/Aids pastoral counselling that OCMS initiated with St Paul's University College, Limuru (Kenya), MAP International and the University of

[7] Alan Nichols represented World Vision Australia in refugee work and was present at the Rwanda border during the 1994 genocide.

[8] Tharcisse Gatwa – a Presbyterian minister in Rwanda who has since written *The Churches in the Rwandan Crisis 1991–1994* published by Regnum Books. Caesar Molebatsi, author of *A Flame for Justice* was a worker among young people in Soweto, South Africa during their freedom struggle.

Wales. Through the First Fruit foundation in California and Global Mapping International, a report was commissioned of that and other church-related programmes, which was presented at the summer school and subsequently disseminated globally by the World Health Organization.

Other special meetings were arranged focusing on South Africa with Caesar Molebatsi; Management and Christian Mission in partnership with Far East Broadcasting Associates led by Dr Mee-Yan Judge; and the launch of Archbishop George Carey's biography in 2004. The Centre also hosted one of the first C.S. Lewis Society conferences in Oxford, and a conference of the St Theosavia Society. As OCMS' own use of the building increased, such use of its facilities for conferences, though financially helpful, decreased.

Attendance numbers at these schools varied between twenty-five and seventy. They were self-sustaining through the fees of the attenders, sometimes raised by scholarship funding, and the generous contribution of the time and travel of the seminar leaders. In this way, the schools did not depend on securing a grant from an established organisation before they could succeed and they became a defining feature of OCMS' work. They set mission agendas by identifying emerging themes in mission, enrolling those who were giving leadership to them, and then disseminating the presentations, reports and results through the journal *Transformation,* which was becoming a journal of record. They also expressed OCMS' way of operating – not to be operational itself but to stimulate and, where possible, enable the operation of others.

There were no precedents for these types of summer schools, which focused on the development and implementation of contextual wholistic theology. We had to make them up for ourselves and learn from our experience.

Development of publishing: *Transformation* and Regnum Books

In 1978, the National Conference on Social Ethics was held at High Leigh. Bruce Nicholls of the World Evangelical Fellowship (WEF)

Theological Commission convened it. John Stott chaired the conference and paid for Vinay Samuel to attend. Vinay was invited to be a member of the Theological Commission and of its Study Unit on Ethics and Society. He worked with the Convenor, Ron Sider, and often as its Chair. The Unit engaged in dialogue with the Lausanne Committee on World Evangelisation on the issues of Evangelism and Social Concern. The Unit on Ethics and Society launched the OCMS journal, *Transformation,* with Ron Sider and Vinay Samuel as editors. Paternoster Press, the Publisher for the WEF, produced it. After ten years, the WEF became uncomfortable with some of the journal's authors and asked Vinay and Ron to find it a new home. Thus, OCMS took on *Transformation* as its publisher.

Paternoster Press had been founded by Howard Mudditt, the son of missionaries to China, and was managed by his son Jeremy. Paternoster and Regnum agreed to publish jointly. Regnum found the authors and produced the manuscript. Paternoster took the manuscript, got the cover designed, got the text ready for printing, printed and distributed. They also fixed the price in consultation with Regnum. They did the marketing and distribution. The proceedings of the Conference on Simple Lifestyle was the first joint publication with the WEF. A colleague of Howard, Paul Broomhall, a grandson of Hudson Taylor, lived in Battle, Sussex. Both were thoughtful supporters of OCMS. Paul managed the Sarangpur Trust, named after a town in Uttar Pradesh, India. Both were part of the many bricks that made up OCMS.

The publication company, Regnum Books, has its roots in the work of Partnership in Mission Asia. Vinay Samuel and Chris, with support from David Bussau (Australia), Jonathan Chao and Wilson Chao (Hong Kong), Melba Maggay and David Lim (Philippines) published a series of leaflets on the theme of gospel and culture; these publications included *Gospel to the Poor, The Gospel and Urbanisation* – especially the urban poor – and *The Gospel and Other Religions.*

The relationship with Andrew Walls, at the University of Aberdeen, developed when Vinay Samuel invited him to help Indian Church History lecturers in their teaching of Church History as part of PIM Asia workshops.[9] One of his research students was Kwame Bediako from Ghana. Andrew was impressed with his work and was keen that it be published, but could not find a publisher to take it on. OCMS published it in 1999. Andrew described it as 'a book of outstanding importance.' [10] Vinay freed up Chris's time to do the editing work. Vinay suggested the title 'Theology and Identity' and Kwame approved.

Publishing through *Transformation* journal and Regnum Books together with the summer schools spread the footprint of transformation theology around the world. OCMS engaged with INFEMIT, which had adopted transformation theology; the WEF – particularly its Unit on Ethics and Society; and attended further consultations of the Lausanne Movement and conferences of the WCC – particularly on the Integrity of Creation. OCMS had a Unique Selling Point of transformation theology. It was non-Western, international and based on a non-Western network of actors rather than a Western institutional organisation.

Our Researchers

Our researchers opened up new fields for the study of mission in the academy. How the gospel became real in different cultures was critically important. One of our first graduates was Daniel Sanchez, a Hispanic American who explored 'an interdisciplinary approach to theological contextualisation with special reference to Hispanic Americans'. He now lectures worldwide on intercultural issues, founding congregations, contextualisation, and ministering in Roman Catholic cultures. He served as Professor of Missions at Southwestern

[9] It was while Vinay was still based in India and, so, possibly between 1989 and 1992.

[10] *Theology and Identity: The impact of cultures on Christian thought in the second century and in modern Africa*, Oxford: Regnum, 1999.

Baptist Theological Seminary in Texas for more than twenty-five years. His interest in worldviews as a prerequisite for effective ministry is reflected, as seen in his thesis and in some of his books – *Church: Church Growth and Culture; Hispanic Realities Impacting America; Sharing the Good News with Roman Catholic Friends; Gospel in the Rosary: Study Guide; and Starting Reproducing Churches: A Guidebook for Contextual New Church Development.*

Such interdisciplinary studies were not necessarily seen as 'kosher' in the academy at the time. It was fascinating and encouraging to discover that senior academics at Oxford University and elsewhere were willing to explore these themes. An early example was Bambang Budijanto, now General Secretary of the Asian Evangelical Alliance. He researched 'Socio-religious values and participation: a comparative study of the processes of value-change in three rural Javanese hamlets and their relationship to people's participation in development.' His supervisor, Dr Marcus Banks, was the Head of the newly created Department of Social (and later Material) Anthropology. His specialism was Indonesian culture, having spent time there. Though not a Christian himself, he was tremendously committed to Bambang's project to research the role of religion in development. He was willing to explore value change due to the faith of the people among three Christian and three Muslim villages in Indonesia with Bambang Budijanto. How did change take place? How did religion make a difference? Bambang himself had to struggle with his use and command of English and so providing language support for him was important. His supervisor recommended his examiners.

While registered with the University of Wales through OCMS, to all intents and purposes Bambang did an Oxford University research degree with access to Oxford libraries and academics. Our researchers not only explored the impact and change which the gospel brought, but also how the Bible is read in different contexts. Andrew Curtis, a Baptist from Australia, looked at how prisoners and prison warders read the gospel of Luke, again supported by

Oxford University supervisors. He is now Founder and Director of the Dragonfly Collective, an international social enterprise consultancy in Australia working to create a more just world. Some did straightforward studies of the biblical text. Augustine Pagolu from India looked at 'Patriarchal religion as portrayed in Genesis 12–50: comparison with ancient Near Eastern and later Israelite religion.' He is now Professor and Head of the Department of Biblical Studies at the South Asian Institute for Advanced Christian Studies and the author of *The Religion of the Patriarchs*. Pam Bendor-Samuel, International Translation Consultant for Summer Institute of Linguistics International and mother of the present director of OCMS, also did biblical studies and stopped with an MPhil, which achieved her purpose.

Among others from the Western world keen to study through OCMS was Gene Early who examined the leadership of an international Christian University under the supervision of Professor Rosemary Stewart, a well-known professor of management studies. He later co-founded Genomic Health, a Silicon Valley molecular diagnostic company and trailblazer in personalised medicine. He brought the neuro-linguistic programming process to Europe. With his PhD in leadership and organisational development, he works as a strategic advisor to global leaders. Another from the USA was Stanley Granberg who investigated African leadership and leadership effectiveness among the Churches of Christ in Meru, Kenya. He served for fifteen years as the director of Kairos Church Planting, a ministry that recruits, trains and supports church planting leaders across the United States. Young-Gi Hong, later President of the Institute of Church Growth in Korea, investigated the nature of charismatic pastoral leadership in the Korean mega-churches.

Malcolm Hunter, author of *To the Ends of the Earth* and *Appropriate Development for Nomadic Pastoralists* examined the value and meaning of wholistic development among the Boran – a nomadic people in Northern Kenya. Pervaiz Sultan, later Principal of St

Thomas' Theological College, Karachi, researched the involvement of the Church of Pakistan in Development and published his work in *Church and Development*. Gideon Githiga researched how the church in Kenya stood up against the authoritarian rulers of Kenya after independence. He later became the first Bishop of Thika and Chair of Five Talents (Kenya), a micro-finance organisation. In mission history, Moo Youl Choi looked at Korean Presbyterianism and social work.

Coralie Joyce from Australia researched the worldviews of Christian communities in Eastern Indonesia and the implications of changing and transitional worldviews for the life and witness of the Christian community. Ladder Myllienmgap from North East India studied the relationship between Christianity and Khasi-Jaintia culture in Meghalaya. Some studies were primarily theological. Sung-Wook Hong studied the theological contextualisation of the concept of God in Korea: naming the Christian God in Korean religious culture. He is now Senior Pastor of First Presbyterian Church in Anyang, Korea, and teaches missiology at various universities. Pentecostals also came to study with OCMS. Doug Petersen, one time President of Latin America Child Care, developed 'A Pentecostal theology of social concern in Central America'. He is now Professor at Vanguard University, California. Damon So from Hong Kong and now a Research Tutor at OCMS looked at Karl Bath's theology of the Trinity from a Chinese perspective, demonstrating a quality equivalent to anything from Oxford and Cambridge, from where his examiners came. Daniel Hardy, a Professor at Cambridge, identified it as a unique contribution to Barthian studies. Samuel Jayakumar from India, now a Professor at Madras Theological Seminary and College, examined the relationship between missionary strategy, Dalit consciousness and socio-economic transformation, and was one of the earliest to look at the conversion of Dalits as an evangelical.

Theological education was another area that was explored. Jonathan Ingleby, a member of the Brethren Church and

Headmaster of a Christian school in India (and subsequently postgraduate lecturer on mission at Redcliffe College, Gloucester), researched Christian missionary education by English Protestant missionaries in India with special reference to cultural change. Bernhard Ott, an Anabaptist from Switzerland, investigated mission training in evangelical Bible colleges and seminaries in Germany and German-speaking Switzerland. He is now Chairman and Accreditation Director of the European Evangelical Accrediting Association (EEAA) and is the Academic Dean of the European School of Culture and Theology, Korntal, Germany. Studies in Islam were undertaken by Len Bartlotti who looked at Islam and the construction of identity among Pashtuns in Pakistan. He describes his current work as an intercultural consultant as awakening people to new possibilities for designing caring and innovative responses to an intercultural world. Mark Beaumont examined Christology in dialogue with Muslims and is currently Director of Postgraduate studies at Birmingham Christian College. Sharon Samson studied the training of semi-literates to teach classes of children in Addis Ababa, Ethiopia, and was enabled to explore the whole area of orality, which was then emerging and has become important in research. She is now Executive Director at International Bible Lessons in Michigan, USA. Also, in the field of religions, Ivan Satyavrata explored the fulfilment concept in the Christian understanding of other religions in Indian Christian thought under the guidance of the senior scholar Julius Lipner. Ivan is Board Chairman of World Vision India and Senior Pastor of the Assembly of God Church in Kolkata, which has close to four thousand people and a significant social outreach, providing education and basic nutrition for several thousand children in and around the city of Kolkata. David Singh looked at Sainthood and Revelatory Discourse. He is a specialist in Islamics, Interfaith and Theology of Religions, and leads the PhD programme at OCMS. Frank Adams' work on the Asante Odwira Festival in Ghana explored something that has the potential of reshaping African Christian liturgy. Dela

Adadevo (Ghana) examined an African understanding of salvation and was commended by his examiners. After establishing a Christian university in Zimbabwe, he moved to political theology and developed a major programme equipping senior African politicians with Christian approaches to public life.

Through Peter Kuzmic and the Evangelical Seminary at Osijek, a number of Romanian scholars studied through OCMS. Christian Romocea, Marcel Macelaru, and Corneliu Constantineanu all wrote excellent theses and contributed much to post-communist East European evangelical/Pentecostal theological development. Christian Romocea is Head of the International Bible Advocacy Centre at the British and Foreign Bible Society. Marcel is now Professor of Theology within the Faculty of Humanities and Social Sciences, the Pentecostal Theology programme. Corneliu's thesis was titled The Social Significance of Reconciliation in Paul's Theology with Particular Reference to the Romanian Context. He was supervised by Miroslav Volf from Yale, a close friend of OCMS. Corneliu became Academic Dean of the Osijek Seminary and sadly died from Covid-19 in 2021.

All of these colleagues did their research while continuing their ministries and struggling with accessing the finances for their studies. We salute them. Our researchers were among the first to do Mission Studies at PhD level and their work defined the discipline of Mission Studies in the British university context. Their studies and others like them set the standard for new areas of academic research. They did not define their topics as research into missionary work but looked at the impact of the engagement of Christians in their societies, and their economic, cultural, religious, political and leadership implications.

Other institutions in the field were the Fuller School of Church Growth and the University of Utrecht. OCMS approached matters differently: it had to prove within the British academy field that Mission Studies was a legitimate discipline. The academy was suspicious of religion and not convinced that it could bring social change. Critical theory dominated social research. Religion was seen purely as a set of (false and possibly oppressive) beliefs. Mission work and its evidence was seen as experience and testimony, not knowledge. Those who brought the change about were the researchers themselves through the quality of their work. They defined what writing mission study research is. They came with the real 'on the ground' challenges that they and their Christian communities faced and sought passionately to get to the bottom of the matter. They enabled Mission Studies to take its place as a discipline equal to any other department in the area of theological studies and developed the ways in which it could be studied and assessed.

Chapter 3

A Movement Adapting to Institutional Life: OCMS 2006–2016[1]

Wonsuk Ma

Introduction

This reflection focuses on the transitional decade after the era of the founding leaders (1983–2006). While continuing its commitment to the vision of wholistic mission based on the evangelical faith, this period marked a new opportunity and challenge for the Oxford Centre for Mission Studies (OCMS) to reposition itself in the changing global and ecumenical context. The reflection also takes the personal perspective of the author.

Since its founding in 1983, OCMS has become the flagship institution advancing the vision of wholistic mission studies (also known as 'integral mission' or 'mission as transformation'), particularly by and for the churches in the Global South. My tenure began in 2006 after the two-decades or so of its existence. The first half of my time was a series of delightful discoveries of the unique vision of OCMS and its cognate network, the International Fellowship of Mission Theologians (INFEMIT) of the Two Thirds World. This reflective recollection focuses on the locus of wholistic mission as put forward by OCMS in the broader and global mission dynamics. We begin with its global Christian context and expounds on three major

[1] An earlier version is to appear as 'The Growing Vision of Holistic Mission: A Reflective Memoir on OCMS in the Changing Global Context (2006–2016),' in The International Missionary Council Centenary Series published by Regnum and due in 2024.

areas of OCMS' engagement with mission networks. My interest is in how its widening engagements affected both OCMS and its partners.

GLOBAL CHRISTIAN CONTEXTS

There are two relevant background themes through which to understand the role of OCMS and its commitment and contribution to wholistic mission studies (HMS): the shift of global Christianity through the twentieth century, and the birth and development of the evangelical mission movement, epitomised by the Lausanne Committee for World Evangelization. The founders' reflections adequately cover the latter topic; my focus here is on the global Christian context during my tenure as OCMS' Executive Director.

The radical shift of global Christianity, for a century since the 1910 Edinburgh Missionary Conference, is statistically presented in the *Atlas of Global Christianity*,[2] a volume published to commemorate the centenary of the conference. In several ways, the period marked the highest watermark in global and Western Christianity: The Christians accounted for 34.8% of the world population,[3] a record high in the two-millennium existence of Christianity. Christians in Europe and North America (or the Global North) claimed 80.9% of the world's Christians.[4] Understandably, 'missionaries' were, by default, Westerners (97.4%).[5]

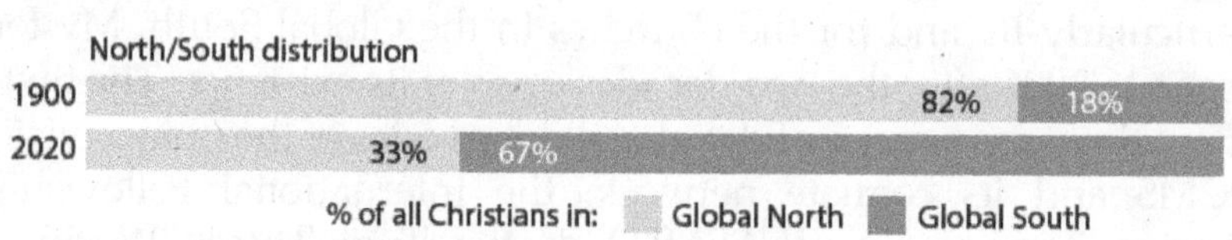

[2] Todd M. Johnson and Kenneth R. Ross, eds., *Atlas of Global Christianity* (Edinburgh: Edinburgh University Press, 2009). The *Atlas* (henceforth) is a publication commemorating the centenary of the Edinburgh Conference.
[3] *Atlas*, 7.
[4] *Atlas*, 8.
[5] *Atlas*, 261.

By 2010, Christianity had shrunk to 33.2% of the world population (from 34.8% in 1910). Europe and North America now accounted for 37.9% of world Christians (from 80.9% in 1910).[6] According to the *Atlas*, the balance of global Christianity tipped toward the South in the early 1980s.[7] As an institution that 'privileges' the Global South, OCMS was born during this historic period and has ridden this global wave.

This radical southward move of global Christianity is not just about the redistribution of the total number of Christians. This is because the redistribution of Christian numbers has profound implications as the editors of the *Atlas* note as follows: 'Southern Christians will interpret and critique Northern Christianity's recent dominance in theology and ecclesiology by producing their own reflections and by looking back to the earliest Christian centuries, when they were in the majority.'[8]

Continuing Agenda of Wholistic Mission

The most significant contribution of OCMS in this context was the birthing and nurturing of the concept of wholistic mission, with its varied expressions and research concerns. There are helpful resources to trace the movement's historical development, including the experiences of the founders of OCMS. It suffices to note that the wholistic mission movement had to battle with fellow evangelicals to establish its legitimacy. The 'mavericks' of wholistic mission had to face charges of being 'liberal' and 'communist.' Within the Lausanne community, they had to survive the ideological tug-of-war with the camp that accorded priority to 'proclamation'.[9]

---

[6] *Atlas*, 7; 8. The chart is from Todd M. Johnson and Gina A. Zurlo, eds., *World Christian Encyclopedia*, 3rd ed. (Edinburgh: Edinburgh University Press, 2019), 4. For a more comprehensive study, see Wonsuk Ma, 'Global Christianity: Where Are We and How Did We Get Here?' *Pentecostal Education* 6, no. 1 (Spring 2021): 35–59.

[7] *Atlas*, 51.

[8] *Atlas*, 8.

[9] Referring to the tension between evangelism and social concern as the Lausanne Covenant states 'Both [evangelism and social concern] are necessary expressions

When I joined OCMS, it had already established formidable programmes to advance wholistic mission studies. OCMS was training one hundred and seven key mission leaders through its graduate and postgraduate programmes, particularly from the Global South. In the 2005–2006 academic year, fifteen new scholars were admitted: eight from Africa (Nigeria, Uganda, Kenya, Tanzania and Zambia), three from Asia (India and South Korea), and three from the US.[10] During the same academic year, fifteen PhD dissertations were examined through three awarding universities (Wales, Open and Leeds Universities).[11] Through its academic programmes, the school produced a new breed of scholar-practitioners. A tangible outcome was evident in the scholars' unique and robust research, mostly involving real-life missionary engagement. OCMS' theses shaped an inimitable category in mission studies. The centre's strategic operation also involved the dissemination of knowledge thus produced through its quarterly journal, *Transformation*, and imprint, Regnum Books. An internal report listed five new Regnum titles published in the 2005–2006 academic year,[12] which was increased to fourteen titles in 2015.[13]

Although OCMS' commitment to wholistic mission studies found itself in an uneasy position within the evangelical mission world, the wholistic mission movement was riding an upward trajectory. The turn of the tide may be attributed to several key activities and trends, such as:

---

of our doctrines of God and Man, our love for our neighbor and our obedience to Jesus Christ.' Lausanne Movement, 'The Lausanne Covenant' (1974, https://lausanne.org/content/covenant/lausanne-covenant#cov), accessed on May 24, 2021. For a helpful historical study, see Al Tizon, *Transformation after Lausanne: Radical Evangelical Mission in Global-Local Perspective* (Oxford: Regnum Books, 2008).

[10] Thomas Harvey, 'Academic Dean's Report to the OCMS Board' (June 2006).

[11] T. Harvey, 'Academic Dean's Report to the OCMS Board' (Dec 2006).

[12] Ibid.

[13] Wonsuk Ma, 'Executive Director's Report to the June 2015 Council of Trustees Meeting' (June 2015).

1. the rise of the churches in the Global South;
2. the activism of high-profiled first-generation 'radical evangelical' figures such as Rene Padilla, David Gitari, Kwame Bediako, Peter Kuzmič, John Stott and others;[14]
3. the studies produced by the leaders and their institutions (such as Bediako's Akrofi-Christaller Institute for Theology, Mission and Culture in Ghana);
4. the growing output of academic research by OCMS; and
5. the growing conscientisation among evangelicals.

The clear evidence of the evangelicals' acceptance of wholistic mission was clear in the 2010 Cape Town Congress of the Lausanne Movement. Many plenary addresses contained wholistic mission approaches in a matter-of-fact manner. Doug Birdsall, the Lausanne's International Director, was completing his PhD study at OCMS on the development of the wholistic mission movement. OCMS organised a volume for the Edinburgh Centenary Series to highlight the contribution of wholistic mission to the global Christian mission movement.[15]

Over the years, the focus of wholistic mission studies was expanded from its initial emphasis on poverty. Two new areas may be worth mentioning. The first is mission cooperation and church unity, the key agenda of the Edinburgh Conference and the International Missionary Council, succeeded by the Commission of World Mission and Evangelism (CWME) of the World Council of Churches (WCC). OCMS' (re)engagement with the broader world church came as it grew confident in its identity and mission. As a more detailed discussion is found below, it suffices to mention the publication of a Regnum title about the Global Christian Forum (GCF), a new ecumenical network, and three Regnum handbooks of

---

[14] David Cranston and Ruth Padilla DeBorst, eds., *Mission as Transformation: Learning from Catalysts* (Oxford: Regnum Books, 2013).

[15] Brian E. Woolnough and Wonsuk Ma, eds., *Holistic Mission: God's Plan for God's People*, RECS 5 (Oxford: Regnum Books, 2010).

theological education initiated by a WCC office. The other is 'nation-building' as a mission agenda. The latter was first advocated by Malaysian Methodist Bishop Hwa Yung, who also served as the Chair of OCMS' Council of Trustees for many years, reflecting the post-colonial realities in Africa, Asia and Latin America, and struggles to reclaim national identities and establish nationhood.[16] An opportunity arose to identify and provide PhD studies to key Christian leaders of South Sudan, the newest independent state in the world. Some had managed a church-based education system, including Muslim-majority Sudan. By the production of new dissertations from the 2000s, OCMS emerged as the largest doctoral mission study programme in Europe after the heydays of the Selly Oaks Colleges and Utrecht University.

INFEMIT transitioned during this time from the founders' generation to a new generation. Now modified as the International Fellowship for Mission as Transformation, its relationship with OCMS changed to that of partner. The understanding of the current leadership of INFEMIT is worth reading:

> *Slowly, INFEMIT began to move into the background, addressing occasional and infrequent opportunities determined by a small team of leadership. By the 21st century, INFEMIT was barely active . Shortly before his death, Kwame Bediako met with Ruth Padilla DeBorst at an OCMS Board meeting and urged her to call together people of her generation to revitalize INFEMIT. She and a handful of others began to explore this possibility, but they were cautious at first.... [However] the relevance of a global fellowship committed to contextual theologies, a holistic understanding of the gospel, and deep scholarship was just as great. So a small group of leaders representative of different regions of the world began meeting periodically, praying and seeking to discern the way forward for a reactivated INFEMIT.*[17]

[16] This agenda was first raised by Bishop Hwa Yung, the Chairman of OCMS Board of Directors at the installation of the younger leaders of INFEMIT.
[17] INFEMIT, 'History,' https://infemit.org/mission/history/, accessed on April 17, 2023.

The 2011 Global Summit of INFEMIT in Nairobi marked its new age, where the founding generation and the younger leaders met. The refreshed relationship between INFEMIT and OCMS was marked by the annual Stott-Bediako Forum, a conference advancing the wholistic mission agenda. The first publication from this partnership was the volume, *Mission as Transformation,*[18] featuring early leaders of INFEMIT such as John Stott, Kwame Bediako, David Gitari, Catharine Padilla, Juan José Barreda, David Bussau, Peter Kuzmič, and Ronald Sider. It was an enriching experience to witness the new INFEMIT leaders, both the founding generation (with Samuel Escobar and Ron Sider) and the new (led by Al Tizon and Ruth Padilla DeBorst), shaping the theme and programme of the 2019 annual meeting of the American Society of Missiology. Al Tizon was the President of this ecumenical society, and the theme was 'Lifestyles of the Rich and Faithful: Stewardship and the Christian Mission.'

Expanding the Engagement Circle

OCMS' widening engagements came at least with the concurrent change of several conditions. The first is the change in the ecumenical world. The birth of the evangelical mission movement caused a self-review among ecumenical mission circles. For example, the CWME, the bastion of ecumenical missiology, decided to invite evangelical and Pentecostal delegates to its thirteenth conference in Athens, Greece (2005). The theme was also carefully selected to accommodate the new delegates' interest: 'Come, Holy Spirit, and Heal and Reconcile.'[19] From participating in the conference, I continued my involvement with the CWME. One significant involvement was the Commission's process in the formulation of its new statement of

[18] David Cranston and Ruth Padilla DeBorst, eds., *Mission as Transformation: Learning from Catalysts* (Oxford: Regnum Books, 2013).
[19] Jacques Matthey, *Come Holy Spirit, Heal and Reconcile! Called in Christ to Be Reconciling and Healing Communities: Report of the WCC Conference on World Mission and Evangelism, Athens, Greece, May 9–16, 2005* (Geneva, Switzerland: WCC Publications, 2008).

mission, 'Together Toward Life,'[20] formally adopted in the WCC's tenth General Assembly in Busan, Korea (2013). The new mission statement shows a considerable effort to recognise evangelical mission concerns,[21] particularly in comparison to the 1982 document, 'Mission and Evangelism: An Ecumenical Affirmation.'[22] OCMS, as a global community committed to mission studies, found these changes conducive to its widening engagements.

The second was the emergence of new global and ecumenical spaces. The GCF was a broad ecumenical camp born out of the realisation that the WCC embraced only about a quarter of the world's Christians. From its 1998 beginning, various preparatory meetings and regional gatherings were held. The Forum began with an ambitious goal to include all the major church traditions: Catholic, Orthodox, historic Protestant, evangelical, Pentecostal, and independent churches. And it has succeeded in this vision: 'To create an open space wherein representatives from a broad range of Christian churches and inter-church organizations … can gather to foster mutual respect, to explore and address together common challenges.'[23] In operational terms, 'From the beginning, there has been a GCF commitment that in its meetings about half of the participants come from those evangelical, Pentecostal, and other churches which have not engaged in the ecumenical movement. The

---

[20] Jooseop Keum, ed., *Together towards Life: Mission and Evangelism in Changing Landscapes* (Geneva: WCC Publications, 2013).

[21] For example, Samuel Escobar, 'Together towards Life: An Evangelical Assessment,' in Kenneth R. Ross et al., eds., *Ecumenical Missiology: Changing Landscapes and New Conceptions of Mission*, RECS 35 (Oxford: Regnum Books, 2016), 429–437.

[22] Its full text is found in '1982 Mission and Evangelism: An Ecumenical Affirmation,' in *Ecumenical Missiology*, 99–125. The volume contains the official documents of ecumenical missiology.

[23] Global Christian Forum, 'Guiding Purpose Statement' (https://globalchristianforum.org/introduction/guiding-purpose-statement/), accessed on May 28, 2021.

other half represents churches historically engaged with the ecumenical movement.'[24]

Equally significant is its relational ethos, where sharing one's journey with Christ has become the main feature of its gatherings.

> *This space is primarily a 'forum'. It is an open space, welcoming representatives of all Christian communities.... At the same time, within the Forum, it is recognised and accepted that the way in which participants affirm this truth may differ.... Participants are therefore invited to engage one another in the challenges – and enriching opportunities – of expanding their ways of understanding, speaking about, and experiencing ecclesial life. They are invited to speak from the integrity of their own perspectives, traditions and experiences. Everyone is to listen respectfully and openly to accounts of the living Word of God at work in the people of God, which may be expressed in ways different to those in which they are accustomed to speaking about their faith.*[25]

Pentecostal practices might have inspired this 'testimony-sharing' method. OCMS participated in and contributed to this groundbreaking effort in various ways. Three teaching staff members attended its first international gathering in Limuru, Kenya (2007) and one in the second gathering in Manado, Indonesia (2011). The Theology Working Group, which I led, produced 'Our Unfolding Journey with Jesus Christ,' and one meeting was held at OCMS. *Transformation* published the Forum's 2007 documents, while Regnum Books published its significant documents and proceedings.[26]

The third was the unique locus of OCMS in global Christianity and its confidence in reaching out broadly. With my own

---

[24] Global Christian Forum, 'Our Unfolding Journey with Jesus Christ: Reflections on the Global Christian Forum Experience' (2013), 2 (https://globalchristianforum.org/wp-content/uploads/2018/07/GFC-Our-Unfolding-Journey-ENG.pdf), accessed on May 28, 2021.

[25] 'Our Unfolding Journey,' 4–5.

[26] Hubert van Beek, ed., *Revisioning Christian Unity: The Global Christian Forum* (Oxford: Regnum Books, 2009).

ecumenical interactions, I was convinced that wholistic mission grounded in the evangelical faith was best positioned to relate with both ecumenical and evangelical mission worlds. I also recognised that for the first three decades, OCMS had prioritised establishing wholistic mission as a legitimate evangelical mission agenda, particularly vis-à-vis the dominance of evangelism/proclamation. The dawn of the twenty-first century marked a new era. The Ecumenical Theological Education Desk of the WCC recognised the 'neutral' nature of OCMS while aware that WCC Publication titles seldom reached evangelical and Pentecostal readers. At that time, the Desk was planning the ambitious publication of a series of theological education handbooks. We had a fruitful conversation where I reassured colleagues that the books would be genuinely 'ecumenical,' duly including chapters on evangelical and Pentecostal theological education. As the leader of the Desk gladly consented, Regnum published massive 'Handbooks on Theological Education and Ecumenism'.[27] Regnum also launched the 'Studies of Global Christianity Series' to publish titles on global Christianity and inter-church concerns. As the interdenominational nature of OCMS gained wide recognition, the community and its publications became a favored space for engagements and exchanges. The summit was reached around the Edinburgh Centenary programmes (as outlined below), even as OCMS continued its development journey through creative ecumenical engagement.

CONVENING AND BROKERING GIFT

Taking a step further, OCMS began exercising its 'neutral' and 'global' identity to become involved in new initiatives actively. I mention three below.

The first is the Global Forum of Theological Educators (GFTE). In the early 2000s, having a new relationship with Dietrich Werner, the Director of the WCC's Ecumenical Theological Education Desk, I

[27] Handbooks have become a new series under the new Regnum leadership: https://www.regnumbooks.net/collections/handbooks, accessed on June 4, 2021.

encouraged Manfred Kohl of Overseas Council International to engage with the former. The ambassador-at-large of this evangelical foundation, facilitating the training of Christian leaders of the Global South, had a positive visit with the WCC leaders in Geneva. Through subsequent meetings with the representatives of major Christian communities, the idea of an ecumenical network of theological educators began to emerge. Its need was set out in the invitation letter to the first international gathering:

> *Most global conversations have been among evangelicals, or among ecumenical or historical Protestants, or among Roman Catholics or among Orthodox, or among indigenous church leaders, but seldom have these conversations been across these ecclesial communities. As the world is changing, as the worldwide shape of Christianity is changing, as Christians in other settings are invited to engage in dialogue with other world religions, as theological schools across the Christian spectrum face ever more similar problems, it becomes increasingly important for theological educators across the Christian spectrum and around the world to know and understand one another.*[28]

It adopted the format developed by the GCF:

> *[t]he goal of the meeting is that theological educators will become better acquainted with one another, engage in conversation about the education of pastors and Christian leaders, and better understand one another's work and context. Focused conversations will include topics such as the treasures we bring to the common table, how theological education forms persons for ministry, integrity and leadership, the contributions that different Christian communities and national contexts bring to Christian theological education, and more.*[29]

The 2015 meeting at OCMS was a decisive point toward the formation and inaugural gathering of the Forum. Its stakeholders

---

[28] Global Forum of Theological Educators, 'The Inaugural Meeting – May 16-20' (an invitation letter, Dec 2015).
[29] 'The Inaugural Meeting.'

spent several days at OCMS: Steve Bevans (Catholic), Daniel Buda (Orthodox), David Esterline (Protestant), Rufus Ositelu (Independent), Rosalee Veloso-Ewell (evangelical), and me (Pentecostal), along with Kohl and Werner. The first international gathering in 2016 saw many OCMS scholars and staff members participate. The second meeting was held in Greece (2019), and the third took place virtually (2021).

The second is the high-profile China Conference (August 2013), organised by Thomas Harvey, OCMS' Academic Dean. The conference brought to Oxford close to fifty Chinese academics in Confucianism, Neo-Socialism, Neo-Liberalism and Christianity, which was a significant accomplishment. Addressing the ideological vacuum in China after the market-driven economy had pushed socialism from daily reality, the four conflicting ideological camps in one place testified to the organisational ingenuity and the institution's maturity. Despite the initial uneasiness among the groups, after the conference, all the participants agreed that such a gathering should be repeated.[30]

The third is the birth of the *Lausanne Global Analysis*, envisioned by Doug Birdsall, International Director of the Lausanne Movement (and an OCMS scholar), and Tom Harvey. Birdsall writes:

> *Our inspiration ... was a conversation I had with David Young, founder of Oxford Analytica, in 2010. David, a committed believer, and I [Birdsall] were discussing the need Christian leaders have for trustworthy, intellectual analysis of the issues before us in today's world. We felt there was a gap between the massive amount of information that surrounds us 24/7, and the ability to process that information and access credible analysis from an evangelical perspective.*

Thus, the vision of the bimonthly semi-academic publication is 'to deliver strategic and credible information and insight from an international network of evangelical analysts so that Christian

[30] A good reflection on the conference and its impact would be highly recommended for the historical study of OCMS.

leaders will be equipped for the task of world evangelization.'[31] Harvey played a key role in transforming the vision into a published reality. As the *Analysis* runs its tenth year, typically containing five or six studies in each issue, the publication appears in English, Spanish, French, Portuguese, and soon also in Korean.

OCMS expanded its ecumenical engagements and began to convene various inter-church gatherings and facilitate the launch of new initiatives to serve the wider church. Such developments resulted from OCMS' self-awareness of its gifts and the affirmation of the outside world.

EDINBURGH 2010

The year 2010, the centenary of the Edinburgh Missionary Conference, was arguably the most significant year for the world of Christian mission. Various celebrations took place: Tokyo Global Mission Consultation (May) among mission organisations, the Edinburgh 2010 Conference (June), the Cape Town Congress of the Lausanne Movement (October), and the Boston Conference (November) among academics.[32]

My wife, Julie, and I were part of the twenty-member 'Toward 2010' Conference (2005), organised by the Church of Scotland to prepare for the centenary of Edinburgh 1910. Our role in the Edinburgh 2010 process was natural after we joined OCMS the following year. The radical change in global Christianity between the original Conference and the centenary celebration was well reflected in its recognition of the differences from 1910:

- Rather than being centred in Edinburgh, a polycentric approach is being taken, both for the study process and for 2010 events

---

[31] 'Publisher's Memo,' *Lausanne Global Analysis* 1:1 (Nov 2012), https://lausanne.org/content/lga/2012-11/2012-11-publishers-memo, accessed on June 3, 2021.

[32] For a study of the four 2010 conferences, see Allen Yeh, *Polycentric Missiology: 21st-Century Mission from Everyone to Everywhere* (Downers Grove, IL: IVP Academic, 2016).

which will take place in many locations around the world including Edinburgh.
- Whereas 1910 was confined to mainline Protestantism, the participants in 2010 are drawn from the whole range of Christian traditions and confessions, including Roman Catholic, Orthodox, Pentecostal, and Independent Churches, and show a better gender and age balance.
- Instead of being confined to the North Atlantic, there is an intentional bias to the South, recognizing that Christianity's centre of gravity has moved markedly southwards during the past century. The process aims to be truly worldwide in its scope.[33]

This (truly) global process was a perfect event for the ecumenically maturing and south-privileging OCMS. Through the various meetings, we learned that the celebration consisted of the study process by the nine commissions, the gathering in Edinburgh, and the publication of various studies.

Studies

The 'Toward 2010' conferences in 2005 and 2006 identified nine study themes (versus eight in 1910):[34]

1. Foundations for mission
2. Christian mission among other faiths
3. Mission and post-modernities
4. Mission and power
5. Forms of missionary engagement
6. Theological education and formation

[33] Centenary of the 1810 World Missionary Conference, 'About Edinburgh 2010' (http://www.edinburgh2010.org/en/about-edinburgh-2010.html), accessed on May 27, 2021.

[34] Centenary of the 1910 World Missionary Conference, 'Main Study Themes' (http://www.edinburgh2010.org/en/study-themes/main-study-themes.html), accessed on June 3, 2021.

7. Christian communities in contemporary contexts
8. Mission and unity – ecclesiology and mission
9. Mission spirituality and authentic discipleship

In addition, seven transversal themes were identified:[35]

1. Women and mission
2. Youth and mission
3. Healing and reconciliation
4. Bible and mission – mission in the Bible
5. Contextualisation, inculturation and dialogue of worldviews
6. Subaltern voices
7. Ecological perspectives on mission

OCMS and the Church Mission Society (CMS, Oxford) jointly hosted the Mission Spirituality study process.[36] Its international consultation in Seoul, Korea, in March 2009 brought a dozen international and ecumenical mission scholars and practitioners with a wide range of case studies. They included: African Instituted Churches; Back to Jerusalem Movement (of the Chinese Church); CMS Africa, including Business as Mission; the Immigrant Church Example; the Russian Orthodox Church; the Pentecostal Church: Korea; the Reformed Church Example; and the Roman Catholic Church in Asia.[37] The interaction among the presenters, hosts, and participants was a rich and challenging learning process. A study commission volume was published to include the final versions of

[35] Centenary of the 1910 World Missionary Conference, 'Study Process – Transversal Topics' (http://www.edinburgh2010.org/en/study-themes/transversal-topics.html), accessed on June 3, 2021.
[36] The study group leaders include Wonsuk Ma (OCMS), Cathy Ross (CMS), Thomas Harvey (OCMS), and Naomi Rose (CMS).
[37] Wonsuk Ma and Cathy Ross, 'Theme Nine: Mission Spirituality and Authentic Discipleship,' in Daryl Balia and Kirsteen Kim, eds., *Edinburgh 2010: Witnessing to Christ Today*, RECS 2 (Oxford: Regnum Books, 2010), 223-36.

the conference studies and commissioned chapters.[38] OCMS also ran another Edinburgh centenary book project on wholistic mission, which was the community's unique contribution to global mission.[39]

Conference (June 2–6, 2010)

The planning and organisation of the conference, initially by the Church of Scotland, spanned from the 'Toward 2010' process to the formation of the General Council. The twenty-member General Council consisted of church communions (Catholic, Orthodox, Pentecostal, African Independent Churches, Baptist, Methodist, Lutheran, Reformed, and Seventh Day Adventist with the Church of Scotland) and global church and mission networks (such as the Lausanne Movement, the WCC, and World Evangelical Alliance).[40] Despite the disappointingly small conference (with only two hundred and fifty delegates and about fifty media observers compared to two thousand in 1910), the diversity and inclusive representation were a stunning achievement of the conference. The Evaluation Report stated:

> *The Edinburgh Conference – was described as one of the most diverse gatherings of the global Church in recent centuries. It enabled dialogue among Christians; opportunities for participants to tell their story; motivating and encouraging worship moments, experienced particularly at the closing celebration; and closer respectful cooperation. There was also some notable local impact with visits to local churches and the interfaith evening.*

---

[38] Wonsuk Ma and Kenneth Ross, eds., *Mission Spirituality and Authentic Discipleship*, Regnum Edinburgh Centenary Series (Oxford: Regnum Books, 2013).
[39] Brian Woolnough and Wonsuk Ma, eds., *Holistic Mission: God's Plan for God's People*, RECS 5 (Oxford: Regnum Books, 2010).
[40] Edinburgh 2010, 'General Council,' 3, items 16, 17 (http://www.edinburgh2010.org/en/about-edinburgh-2010/governance/general-council.html), accessed June 4, 2021.

It is worth noting at this point the statistics of those attending – 300 delegates from 202 organisations/bodies; 115 denominations; 75 nationalities.[41]

Julie Ma, an OCMS Research Tutor, served as a General Council and Executive Council member, actively contributing to the planning, and managing all aspects of the celebration. As the representative of the world's Pentecostal family, she identified various Pentecostal speakers and presenters (both plenary and parallel sessions). I also participated in the planning meetings as an unofficial member, representing Regnum Books, the publisher of the Edinburgh 2010 Conference and study material. Several OCMS scholars attended the conference. Andrew Anderson, the Chair of the Council, joined OCMS after his retirement as the (volunteer) Chaplain and his wife, Hazel, as OCMS' (volunteer) archivist.

Personally, two moments at the conference excited me: Seeing the delegates receive the two conference volumes published by Regnum; and Julie Ma reading a section of the historic Common Call at the closing ceremony held in the General Assembly Hall of the Church of Scotland, the historic venue of the 1910 World Missionary Conference. OCMS had played a notable role.

Publication of the Regnum Edinburgh Centenary Series

Arguably, the most significant contribution of OCMS was the publication of the Edinburgh 2010 studies and conference documents. As the General Council was searching for an ecclesiastically neutral global publisher, OCMS/Regnum soon surfaced in the discussion. Delighted to be asked, my immediate question concerned the capacity: could Regnum handle the task? The publishing operation had just drastically transitioned from one or two titles per year under Paternoster's auspices to the operation run entirely in-house by

[41] Edinburgh 2010, 'Evaluation Report' (http://www.edinburgh2010.org/fileadmin/Evaluation_Report.doc), accessed on June 4, 2021.

OCMS. In 2008, Regnum Books published six titles, an ambitious growth but with shoestring resources.[42]

Regnum initially agreed to publish two conference volumes[43] and possibly a post-conference title.[44] The Chair of the General Council estimated eight titles at the most. A four-member editorial board was established: Knud Jorgensen (Areopagos, Norway), Kirsteen Kim (Leeds, Trinity), Wonsuk Ma, and Tony Gray (Regnum Production Editor). The committee worked long after the General Council had been dissolved. With no ongoing budget, none imagined the series would grow to thirty-five fully financed titles.

In addition to the three conference volumes, most main themes and several transversal topics appeared in the series. Also added were studies of ecclesial bodies, mission movements, and geographical studies. Two compendium volumes also appeared in 2018.

Thanks to the dedicated work of the committee, the willingness of mission communities to spearhead study projects and the financial generosity of the partners, the series emerged as the most extensive collection of mission studies, covering the most extensive ecclesial and geographical ranges.

A celebration was held in 2016 to mark the completion of the series. Many commented that OCMS had punched far above its weight. The series was awarded Mission Books of the Decade by the International Bulletin for Mission Research in April 2020. The Editorial Team donated the whole series to twenty-six global libraries and offered a subsidy to fifty libraries. In the end, Regnum and OCMS made an unprecedented decision to make the full texts of the series available for free download[45] which was warmly

---

[42] W. Ma, 'Executive Director's Report to the Council of Trustees' (June 2008).

[43] David A. Kerr and Kenneth R. Ross, eds., *Edinburgh 2010: Mission Then and Now*, RECS 1 (Oxford: Regnum Books, 2009); and *Edinburgh 2010: Witnessing to Christ Today*.

[44] Kirsteen Kim and Andrew Anderson, eds., *Edinburgh 2010: Mission Today and Tomorrow*, RECS 3 (2011).

[45] www.ocms.ac.uk/free-book-resources/.

welcomed, particularly by individuals and institutions in the Global South. Through the process, Regnum Books (as well as OCMS) emerged as a powerhouse in knowledge creation and sharing for mission.

OCMS Viewed through a Personal Event

December of 2010 closed this eventful year, but a significant and painful personal event was unfolding, affecting the whole community considerably. Julie and I had developed a prayer habit for each evening to intercede for the financial provision for OCMS. As the archive's report indicates, 'Many times, in the past 39 years, OCMS has faced the possibility of closure or dissolution, but always there has been a reprieve, and a new impetus. This has happened because of reliance on God's grace and the guiding of His Holy Spirit.'[46]

In the middle of our nightly prayer, Julie collapsed and remained unconscious. She was rushed to the emergency room and diagnosed with a severe brain aneurysm. The OCMS family sprang into a season of prayer while Deborah Lake, the newly hired Development Officer, desperately spread her updates with a plea for prayers through social media. While Julie was fighting for her life, the OCMS family waged a spiritual war. Julie's illness seemed to us as direct spiritual opposition to the growth and development of OCMS. Each day, the St Philip and St James Church building became a Korean-style prayer revival, firmly believing in God's goodness and power to heal. To the surprise of Julie's medical team, she came out of the induced coma in eight days, began her rehabilitation process in two months, and eventually returned to her supervisory duty. This personal tragedy, occurring at the halfway point in my tenure, affected the community in two specific ways.

The first was the spiritual impact. OCMS was a spiritual family, a community of faith and mission. Some members had led daily

[46] The precarious nature of the institutional operation is well observed by the archiver's report, Hazel Anderson, 'The OCMS Archive' (unpublished presentation delivered to the OCMS community, November 2022), 5.

prayers when we joined OCMS. The prayers for Julie, however, were more than supplications; they almost claimed God's miracle of healing. The community operated on a different level of faith and expectation. A prayer made with sincere expectations transforms passive waiting into active seeking for outcomes. Everyone witnessed the miraculous recovery of Julie. When Brian Woolnough had a heart attack in the building, not only did Deborah Lake perform CPR until an ambulance arrived, the whole community poured out their heartfelt prayers to God for his complete healing. God honored our prayers and met our expectations. This spiritual transformation, I believe, ushered in the next half of my tenure.

The second is the new season of God's provision. The updates on Julie's progressive healing were regularly shared by OCMS with donors and partners. An existing partner in California decided to contribute for two years before finally ending their relationship with OCMS. The most significant development was with Don Chang of Forever 21 of California. The relationship with this Korean-American Christian philanthropist had been nurtured for years, but the substantive contact occurred in Cape Town at the Lausanne gathering in the same year. Julie and I also attended the November opening of his stores in Birmingham and Dublin. He had visited OCMS and had met with the staff. The news of Julie's illness was a shock to him. He immediately decided to become a major supporter of OCMS. Over four or five years, he donated about 1.5 million US dollars for scholarships and the OCMS gallery construction. Around this time, several other donors were also added. Through the gracious work of Bishop Hwa Yung of Malaysia, Mr Lee Oi Hian became a faithful major donor. Also, two megachurches in Korea provided annual gifts to establish two academic Chairs: David Yonggi Cho, Chair by Dr Younghoon Lee of Yoido Full Gospel Church; and Sundo Kim Chair by Dr Chungsuk Kim of Kwanglim Methodist Church.

CONCLUSION

In retrospect, the year 2010 was a watershed point for OCMS' global and ecumenical engagement. The critical role which OCMS and INFEMIT played in the Lausanne's Cape Town Congress in October of the same year was the continuation of its Edinburgh engagement. In closing, I would like to share the following personal reflections.

First, after the 2010 events, I sensed that the conditions were ripe for testing a joint research project involving major global Christian communities. 'Flourishing of life' had been the central theme of the ecumenical mission thinking, well testified in the 'Together towards Life' document. The (Radical) evangelicals, championed by the OCMS–INFEMIT network, had successfully established wholistic mission and the Pentecostals had demonstrated their spiritual capital for the welfare of life, observed as the upward social mobility in Latin America[47] or more derogatively known as the prosperity gospel.[48] As a continuation project, I began an initial conversation with the Secretary of the CWME, which yielded a positive response. While leading OCMS, other priorities prevented me from moving the concept forward. Nonetheless, the idea of bringing together ecumenical and wholistic mission with Pentecostal spirituality reflected the growing confidence and convening influence of OCMS on a global scale.

Second, I felt the timing was God's providence. With the radically different awareness of the global church in a century, the Lord led us to participate in and contribute to the 2010 events. OCMS had reached the maturity and confidence to respond to various opportunities by then. The unique tools, such as Regnum Books, that the OCMS founders had created and developed, were available to the ecumenical and mission partners. Also, my existing

---

[47] David Martin, *Tongues of Fire: The Explosion of Protestantism in Latin America* (Oxford: Blackwell, 1993).

[48] For example, Wonsuk Ma, 'David Yonggi Cho's Theology of Blessing: Basis, Legitimacy, and Limitations,' *Evangelical Review of Theology* 35, no. 2 (April 2011): 140–59.

relationships with various ecumenical networks found the community's readiness to move forward ecumenically. It took a good dose of risk-taking to undertake the massive publication programme of the Edinburgh 2010 Centenary Series, through which the OCMS community learnt that our God was able to provide for those who believed in Him.

Third, as I look back (and also during my tenure at OCMS), I constantly ask myself several questions: Did OCMS and I carefully plan to ride the 2010 wave? Did we know it was coming? Did we take, for example, ecumenism as a mission subject? My answer is a 'yes' in practice, but a 'no' in articulation. It involved learning from OCMS' changing context and exploring various options as a community. I understood that a new leader in my place needed to remain connected with the community's past while also seeking OCMS' expansion. For this, I hoped for a new leader with proper training and experience in organisational leadership, and OCMS got one.

Before I close this reflective memoir, I need to mention one special INFEMIT/OCMS leader who exercised critical leadership albeit often behind the scenes. Bishop Hwa Yung of the Malaysian Methodist Church was responsible for recruiting several OCMS leaders. My move to Oxford began with a working lunch with him in Malaysia. Thomas Harvey, the Academic Dean, joined OCMS through his mediation, and also the Executive Director, Paul Bendor-Samuel. Hwa Yung worked closely with me as the Chair of the Board and the crucial link between the founding and the appointment of new leaders of INFEMIT. He recruited a major donor from his circle after I challenged him by asking, 'Why don't I see any donation from Malaysia?'

Throughout this journey, I witnessed OCMS grow in maturity, and God's Kingdom expand. For this, I am grateful to the community and God, our Master!

CHAPTER 4

GROWING FRUITFULNESS: OCMS' JOURNEY FROM 2016

PAUL BENDOR-SAMUEL

In the decade from 2006 to 2016, Wonsuk Ma consolidated and developed the Oxford Centre for Mission Studies (OCMS) in a number of ways.

The Board decision in 2006 to drop the MA programme and focus on the PhD bore fruit. The PhD cohort grew to around one hundred and twenty, and the programme itself provided a unique approach through primarily part-time study with scholars remaining located in their own ministries and contexts with short annual residencies in Oxford. Around one hundred and sixty supervisors provided specialist content guidance. Their diverse expertise allowed OCMS to tailor the programme to the mission interest of each student. Ma also established Regnum Books as a serious academic mission publisher, working in close collaboration with Tony Gray. Theologically trained, Tony ran his own publishing business and partnered with Regnum for the production aspects of publishing. The PhD programme and publishing strengthened OCMS' reputation in mission studies circles globally. Ma's other major contribution was to not simply engage with but build relationships with ecumenical partners. OCMS retained its evangelical convictions while participating in a wide range of Christian traditions. This not only included the World Council of Churches but also the Global Forum of Theological Educators (GFTE) and

Global Christian Forum (GCF). Ma was a leading contributor to both GFTE and GCF.

My appointment in 2016 provided an opportunity for OCMS to step back and review its vision and mission. The church, and its diverse contexts, had changed dramatically since the formation of OCMS in 1983. Opportunities for theological formation were now widely available in the majority world. The questions I wrestled with were: what in the OCMS ethos and 'DNA' needed to be stewarded into the future; how should we capture this in the vision and mission of OCMS; and where did we need to innovate in order to better fulfil our mission and vision?

Framing OCMS' Distinctive Calling and Mission

We launched a one-year consultative review process, with the aim of clarifying our vision and mission. This review involved the wide range of OCMS stakeholders including the Board, past and present staff, scholars and alumni, and companions who had journeyed with us over the years. Following the analysis of surveys and a number of workshops with staff and the Board, new vision and mission statements were agreed in mid-2017:

> *Our vision: The global church equipped to participate in the realisation of God's transforming mission through research and applied scholarship.*
>
> *Our mission: To advance study, education and research in God's mission and to convene practitioners, scholars and leaders in creative and prophetic dialogue.*
>
> *We do this by:*
>
> - *equipping individuals, leaders, churches and institutions, prioritising those on the cutting edge of God's transforming mission*
> - *responding to issues identified by the church with timely, strategic and rigorous research*
> - *fostering spaces where scholarship and practice interface for mutual learning*

- *ensuring the fruit of scholarship is accessible to reflective mission practitioners*
- *seeking to hear and give voice to reflective practitioners who might otherwise not be heard*
- *working in partnership with like-minded individuals and institutions*

The six key thrusts give expression to the missional intent of OCMS: equipping, research, dissemination of knowledge, connecting, amplifying the voices of those less heard, and partnership. They have proved the basis for repeated interrogation of what more we could do to effectively fulfil our vision and mission, and respond to the needs of reflective mission practitioners and potential scholar-leaders.

It is notable that while the language of Mission as Transformation remains central, our focus now unambiguously became the global church, recognising that increasingly secularised, post-Christian contexts are in as much need of renewed mission theology and practice as anywhere else. A bias towards the majority world was nonetheless retained through our commitment to 'hear and give voice to reflective practitioners who might otherwise not be heard.' This bias shows up in all OCMS programmes, and in those with whom we seek to partner.

In 2019, the Board added a Faith and Ethos Statement, building on the Statement of Faith that appears in our articles of incorporation. The new statement aimed to use more accessible language, while retaining the orthodox Christian position of OCMS combined with the radicalism that is integrally linked to understanding God's mission through the lens of the transformation of individuals, communities and the whole created order. The statement reflects a gracious and open orthodoxy that seeks to demonstrate faith through radical discipleship. The 'ethos' element of the statement is a clear call beyond intellectual convictions to ethical commitments: 'to embody the Gospel of the Kingdom of God in every part of our own lives.'[1]

Most recently, through a couple of staff workshops, a values statement was developed and agreed by the Board in its December 2022 meeting. The Values Statement is a powerful expression of what makes OCMS what it is. It reflects the historic values that have underpinned the organisation while at the same time capturing our aspiration to give richer expression to them. It is worth reproducing them in full:

OCMS is:

1. ***God-Dependent, Christ-Centred, Spirit-Empowered:*** *we are centred on worship, prayer and the Word of God that shape our calling to sacrificial service*

2. ***Globally connected:*** *we seek to embrace diverse expressions of the Body of Christ in companionship and collaboration*

3. ***Hospitable:*** *we aspire to be an open, humble and welcoming community that champions voices less heard*

4. ***Pursuing excellence:*** *we seek God's wisdom to be the best we can as an organisation and in the curiosity and rigour of our research and scholarship*

5. ***Transformational:*** *pioneering and prophetic, and ready to be challenged ourselves, we seek to be and to nurture agents of change at the cutting edges of God's mission.*

---

[1] https://www.ocms.ac.uk/statement-of-faith-and-ethics/ (accessed 04 May 2023).

Putting the Vision and Mission Statements to Work

The renewed vision and mission statements agreed in 2017 released us to explore new opportunities. How else, apart from PhD and publishing, might OCMS fulfil its vision? Some initiatives did not bear fruit. For example, we offered consultancy to mission-related ministries. One organisation wanted to evaluate the impact of its programmes but pulled out at the rigorous approach proposed. The concept worked better when Operation Mobilisation asked us to help them understand what was happening at the intersection of community-based ministries and evangelism in contexts of hostility to the gospel. OCMS facilitated a workshop with a dozen of their more experienced workers out of which they identified ten overarching principles. The workshop led to the publication of *Undivided Witness: Jesus Followers, Community Development and Least Reached Communities.*[2]

Equipping

We continued to receive periodic requests to run an MA programme. Given these are widely available globally through many theological institutions, we continue to believe this is not a priority for OCMS. Nonetheless, the question remained whether the PhD should be our only programme for equipping Christian leaders. This led to the development of two distinctive offers: the Integrated Mission Leadership programme (IML) (of which more later) and the Guided Research Programme (GRP).

In 2018, I was in Hong Kong seeking new sources of funding, and met up with one of our PhD students. The encounter proved to be the most fruitful outcome of the trip. Cary Clifton had spent more than twenty years in non-formal theological education alongside mainland Chinese pastors who had no more than a few years of primary education. As we talked, I asked Cary, 'Do you really need a PhD?' 'No,' he replied, 'I just want help in doing research that will enable me to develop more effective tools for adult education in my

---

[2] David Greenlee, Mark Galpin and Paul Bendor-Samuel (eds) (Oxford: Regnum Books, 2020).

context.' My response was to work with him to design a programme that would meet his need, and Cary became the first scholar in the GRP.

The programme took off when Mark Oxbrow retired from his work leading the Faith2Share network and joined the OCMS faculty. The programme reflects many of the core concerns of OCMS: focused on practice, academically robust, flexible, part-time, guided by a content specialist, and a bias to support those from the majority world. Unexpectedly, we have found that a number have joined having gained their doctorate, and are now wanting postdoctoral experience.

Disseminating knowledge

Interrogation of our approach to publishing with our renewed mission statement led to the launch of two new Regnum Books series. We asked how we might better platform the voices of those less easily heard. With English remaining the dominant language of mission theology and practice, we launched the Global Voices series. We translate into English missiological work that has been published in other languages and reflects contextual concerns and perspectives. Global Voices from Latin America now offers the Global Church a dozen titles. The first, from a Korean context, will be published this year. The concept is now being used as a vehicle for those writing from a Muslim background.

While Regnum Books is a serious academic publisher, our desire is to see the church in its very different contexts equipped for more fruitful and faithful witness. The trickle-down of academic knowledge can be very slow or simply not happen. How could we make the work of our scholars accessible to busy, thoughtful Christians? We discussed stripping a thesis down to fifty pages of essential content, presented in a readable and non-academic way. David Cranston, Chair of the Board, volunteered to have a go. When the manuscript was sent to the author of the PhD, he could not believe it. There are now twenty-four volumes in the series and counting!

In 2009, an agreement was made with Sage to publish *Transformation*, the OCMS' peer-reviewed journal. That agreement was recently renewed for the third time. Nearly ten thousand institutions now subscribe to *Transformation* globally, with seventy per cent of them in the majority world. Since the Covid-19 pandemic, we have seen a significant increase in its use, and in 2022 there were over eighty thousand whole-text downloads.

Leveraging Connection

In 2018, during a Board conversation about the degree to which OCMS research is strategic, the suggestion was made to leverage our reputation and connections and call together a symposium of mission research institutions to share who is focused on what. On further reflection, there seemed limited value in sharing current interests in a one-off event and the idea for a mission research platform was born. With a commitment to partnership and supporting those in the majority world, a consultation was called and sixteen institutions representing each continent gathered in Oxford. This gave rise to the Alliance of Mission Researchers and Institutions (AMRI). Four years later, AMRIConnect was launched (www.amriconnect.net). The platform supports the upload of mission-related scholarship and research but it has additional features designed to enable participants and institutions to connect, create communities and collaborate. Unlike other platforms such as academia.edu, AMRIConnect was launched in eight major languages, and participants can join for free.

The Virtual Pivot

When the Covid-19 pandemic broke out in early 2020, OCMS, in common with other educational establishments, was obliged to pivot rapidly to a virtual delivery mode. At once, mentoring, supervision and support for scholars had to go on line. Prayer meeting, chapel, Montagu Barker lectures, student seminars, staff meetings, and examinations became virtual. While the learning curve was steep and demanding, the Covid legacy for OCMS has been overwhelmingly positive. As online meetings became normative, so the faculty has grown in their support for distance-learning scholars. Regular meetings are now hybrid, enabling those outside Oxford to join chapel, lectures and student seminars. While Covid was tough for some scholars, especially those in the early stages of learning, we have also experienced unprecedented rates of completion.

Montagu Barker endowed the Tuesday academic lecture. In 2019, the Academic Dean, Tom Harvey, took over leadership of the programme and transformed it through the introduction of themed series. By going virtual and then hybrid, the range of speakers has broadened as they need no longer be present in person in Oxford, and the number of attendees beyond the OCMS community has increased greatly.

Bringing Focus through Strategic Intentions

In 2020, with the number of initiatives growing, the senior team worked with the Council to identify a set of Strategic Intentions that could guide the focus of OCMS' development in this season of opportunity. This developed into a set of nine Intentions.

The choice of descriptor was deliberate. At the 1999 Iguassu Consultation, Samuel Escobar coined the phrase 'managerial missiology' to describe a process whereby we engage in God's work primarily through the creation of strategies, techniques and use of corporate management tools. In thinking strategically about the direction of OCMS, we seek to use the best wisdom of organisational development while keeping central practices that nurture dependence on God. Part of this means we hold our plans lightly. We recognise that while we believe God is calling us to certain priorities, these are kept constantly under review and open to change.

The current Strategic Intentions include a number that aim to strengthen the support structures and processes of OCMS. In addition, four key outward facing ministry intentions were agreed.

Existing programmes: *The continual development and improvement of OCMS' existing programmes*

There is no intention to drop what we currently do but rather to seek their continual improvement. A couple of examples from the PhD programme may help.

Starting with a joint seminar with John Stott and Langham Partners, the PhD programme has witnessed a number of different induction processes. In 2020, a totally revised approach was adopted, built around learning modules using a flipped earning approach. A month-long online introductory phase is followed by a five-week in-person residency. A third phase provides for periodic inputs according to the needs of scholars. A modified version of the induction is also offered to GRP scholars.

Around the same time, the decision was made to reduce the scale of the PhD programme. With over one hundred and twenty scholars in the cohort, the programme consumed almost all of the time and financial resources of the institution. Reducing the cohort to around eighty/eighty five has had a number of clear gains. It has allowed for a more rigorous selection process against admission criteria including gender, age, leadership influence and potential missional impact of the research. Now that the cohort has reached its planned size, we are in a position to invest in new initiatives. One of these is driving proactive research.

Proactive research: *The development of OCMS capacity and capability to drive agile, responsive, prophetic mission research focused on strategic global issues.*

One of the undoubted strengths of OCMS is that the research done by our PhD and GRP scholars is not determined by the priorities of faculty based in Oxford. Student research represents the needs and concerns of those living and ministering in very diverse contexts, whether that be the endemic violence of Northern Nigeria; local mission leadership in the Philippines or the place of the church in the public square in secular Canada. The weakness of this approach to research is that it rarely leads to continued research in a strategic area faced by the church.

Alongside OCMS' responsive approach to research, we now need to develop longer-term, in-depth, funded research focused on a few strategic issues. The time is ripe for the launch of the OCMS Research Institute. Attempts have been made to move in this direction. In 2020, we developed the Forum for Faithful Witness, an online hub designed to bring together scholars with a common research interest from different parts of the world. A single research group has been active since 2021, exploring aspects of missional leadership. We have also developed the concept documents to guide the development of OCMS-led research clusters. Despite these initiatives, we have failed to gain momentum. In significant measure, this has been due to the lack of dedicated leadership and faculty time. The appointment of an OCMS Director of Research will be key to developing this wing of OCMS activity that complements our commitment to equipping leaders and supporting individual research.

Integral to the development of OCMS-led research will be the development of the capacity to move beyond the dissemination of knowledge through publication to the 'translation' of the research into accessible knowledge and practical action. OCMS should be well placed ideologically to do this work given its long commitment to bringing practitioners and academics into conversation for mutual learning.

Institutional development: *An emerging global network of mission study centres that reflects OCMS' ethos, working collaboratively to build mission research capability and capacity in service of the global church.*

Since its birth, OCMS has enjoyed relationships with theological centres all over the world. In some cases, this has led to written agreements to support the development of faculty from those institutions, primarily through the PhD programme. OCMS' impact has largely been felt up to this point through the individuals it has supported. Our alumni currently include over one hundred and seventy-five PhD, close to twenty MPhil, seventeen GRP, over fifty IML graduates, and numerous MA students. This is a considerable investment.

OCMS was established to enable Christian leaders to do the kind of research and scholarship that would strengthen the witness and work of the church in the majority world. Forty years on, despite the growth of hundreds of theological institutions, there remain few mission study centres that share the vision, ethos and capacity of OCMS to support rigorous mission scholarship and research. While access to theological study has been democratised across the global church, the capacity to develop mission research remains firmly anchored in North America and Europe. As long as this situation persists, it will be difficult for many in the majority world to have access to equipping in mission scholarship, which in turn limits the voice of the churches in Asia, Africa and Latin America to influence mission discourse. Therefore, it must be a priority for OCMS not only to invest in individual leaders but also to grow partnerships with like-minded institutions, particularly in the majority world, in order to build a network of mutually supporting mission research communities.

Intercultural mission: *An intentional focus on resourcing global mission movements and their leaders*

The nineteenth century saw the flowering of the Euro-American cross-cultural mission movement that had begun in the late eighteenth century. It was a movement that framed mission in territorial terms, depended on an elite force of 'missionaries', understood mission as the responsibility of the church, and saw the goal of mission as planting churches, usually in the image of the church that sent the missionaries.[3] While some, particularly in the World Council of Churches, anticipated its death following the demise of European

[3] See Alan and Eleanor Kreider, Mission and Worship After Christendom (Paternoster, Milton Keynes, 2009).

colonialism, the reverse has happened. Newer mission movements have emerged from the contexts that were once the recipients of missionaries. The 'Christendom' paradigm of mission remains highly influential in shaping the way many still understand mission.

Whatever its flaws, and there were many, it is clear that God has used the Protestant mission movement in remarkable ways, including the birth of new churches across much of Latin America, Africa and Asia. As Robert Woodberry, currently at Baylor University, has ably demonstrated, it also left a transformational impact on societies, particularly in the areas of health and education. Today, mission is increasingly understood as the work of the Triune God whose ultimate purpose is the bringing together in reconciled relationship of all things in heaven and earth under the Lordship of Christ (Eph. 1:10). The King has established his Kingdom and now commands us to participate in it through the communal, integrated witness of localised expressions of the Body of Christ, and through the prophetic word and action of the people of God in every corner of human activity.

The founders of OCMS were more focused on the equipping of church and mission leaders in the majority world to develop their mission theology and practice and less engaged with the changing nature of the mission movement itself. It was perhaps not surprising that with a twenty-five-year background in cross-cultural mission, I brought to OCMS a concern to help mission leaders negotiate the changing nature of cross-cultural mission. This led to the launch of the IML programme, with Mee-Yan Judge as Dean of a faculty focused on four areas: spiritual formation, leadership development, organisational development, and mission. Twenty-three leaders participated in the first cohort, between them representing more than twenty thousand cross-cultural workers. While the core IML programme continues, it has been adapted for shaping leadership within a large mission agency, and plans are in place to bring the programme to different regions globally.

Capacity Building

In order to sustain a diverse portfolio of programmes, the internal capacity of OCMS has been strengthened. The appointment David Brunt as Chief Operating Officer in early 2020 enabled OCMS to make the virtual pivot in response to the Covid-19 pandemic as well as putting in place better financial, administrative, and personnel systems and processes. In the coming years, OCMS must grow its communications and funding sustainability. Over its forty-year history, OCMS has been highly dependent on a few major donors. These have changed over time and we rejoice in God's goodness in providing for the needs of the organisation. It is vital that a broader base of regular financial supporters is developed.

St Philips and St James has provided a distinctive space in the heart of Oxford. Its aesthetic beauty and the sympathetic way in which successive developments have attempted to provide for OCMS as a mission research centre, move all who enter the church. For more than ten years, it has been clear that the current space does not adequately meet the needs of OCMS. Among the constraints are poor heating and lighting, inadequate workspace for staff, limited study carrels for scholars, inadequate hospitality areas and poor reception area. In addition, the fabric of the Grade 1 listed building needs considerable investment. In 2015, Wonsuk Ma was able to get planning permission for a modest north-side extension, and new floors in the south and north transepts. The south transept floor was completed in 2016, ensuring the planning permission remains active.

In 2018, the Board agreed a process to identify the spatial needs of OCMS in the light of its increased diversity of programmes. Following agreement on the development brief, a lengthy process of negotiation ensued with Historic England who eventually reached a position of full support of our proposals. Initially, the city planners appeared similarly sympathetic but, in November 2022, concluded that they would not allow any development that went beyond the 2015 extant permission. Exploration of alternative sites in Oxford had already begun in April 2022 but, by early 2023, it was clear that the long and winding road led back to the door of St Philips and St James. It seems this distinctive building is to remain the home of OCMS for the foreseeable future and we will need to find a way to make it work through a staged, modest development. The vision remains for the site in Oxford to function as a hospitable, inspiring and effective global hub for mission research and scholarship.

CONCLUDING REFLECTION

Over the years, OCMS has gone through various phases of organisational life: initially entrepreneurial, creative and disruptive. This was followed by a period of consolidation, establishing reliability, reputation and connection, and now it is enjoying a phase of multiplication as it builds on the ethos, values and imagination of all that has gone before. What will stop OCMS from simply becoming settled in what it does well and in so doing become increasingly risk-averse? We frequently speak of OCMS as a *'spiritual, missional and academic community.'* It is the holding of these three elements together in creative tension that will allow OCMS to steward the deposit God has placed in us while remaining alive to the work of the Spirit in new ways. These three – spiritual, missional and academic – can be understood through the description of three kinds of spaces: third, thick and thin. Let me conclude this chapter with a brief comment on each of the three.

Third Space

Our founders and their collaborators forged a different way of understanding the mission of God. They could neither accept the narrowness of Western evangelical fundamentalism, nor the shallowness and secularity of Western liberalism. Instead, they pioneered a 'third way,' which held to the authority and reliability of biblical revelation and at the same time took seriously the contexts, cultures and experiences of the growing churches of the majority world. This third way became a third space into which people from very different traditions could engage and be heard.

Third space can be conceived of in two ways. Different parties in dialogue can agree to step out of their own space and join with others in a third space in which respect, listening, and journeying together are valued. Participants do not leave behind their positionality but commit to a posture of openness to the other. OCMS has been creating those kinds of spaces in a number of areas: evangelical and those of other Christian traditions; practitioner and academic; Western and majority world; male and female. Time-consuming and costly, this work is at the heart of OCMS' calling. In a world divided by vicious polarisations, OCMS must continue intentionally to nurture third spaces.

Third space can also be applied to people: third space people. We not only *create* third space but we *are* third space, individually and as a community. For example, third culture kids have been described as third space people. Such people are comfortable with themselves and clear on their own positionality. They are winsome, respectful, and patient. They combine influence with relationship. This is what we mean by the OCMS value of hospitality. We must nurture a community that grows this kind of hospitality and seek to recruit staff who reflect third space by who they are, and create third space for others.

Thick Space

Here I am drawing on the widely used sociological concept of society as 'space' combined with what Clifford Geertz popularised as 'think description', to study what is going on in a community. Geertz emphasised that anthropological study could not rest on outsider perspectives but that sense making required the actors' voice in their context. OCMS has strongly advocated for research that is conceived and driven by practitioner-scholars working in their own context. Much mission research rests on gathering and interpreting quantitative data; research that relies purely on statistical data-gathering risks producing superficial answers. Does the fact that over ninety per cent of Kenyans state Christian as their religious affiliation mean that the Kenyan church is strong and providing a faithful and relevant witness in its national context? Does the fact that barely three per cent of peninsula Malaysia is Christian mean that the church there is weak?

OCMS must maintain a commitment to quality academic research and scholarship. No doubt, OCMS needs to grow its ability to lead research that makes use of quantitative and 'big' data. This will complement our traditional strength, which has been rigorous qualitative, contextual and locally-driven research. As stated earlier, we must grow our capacity to engage in agile, relevant, cutting-edge research that provides a prophetic voice to the church.

The Kingdom of God affirms elements in all cultures while judging all. Mission research seeks to understand how God is at work in our world today. It must also bring into the light works of darkness and spiritual strongholds that hold people captive. If mission involves the proclamation of the Kingdom of God and witness to the total Lordship of Jesus Christ, it is inevitable that mission researchers are engaged in spiritual warfare. I suggest that there is a danger that we settle for 'comfortable' research that is interesting but safe. We cannot retreat from the hard, complex, painful cutting edges of mission today. What will keep us engaged in costly – at times unpopular – mission research? Part of the answer lies with OCMS as thin space.

Thin Space

Thin space is used in some spiritual traditions to describe places or moments when the gap between heaven and earth seems to narrow and the presence of God becomes tangible in a heightened sense. Celtic spirituality strongly affirmed the presence of God in the natural world and drew on the belief that God's presence could be especially felt in certain locations. In what sense might OCMS be a thin space?

Preceding our missional and academic commitments, OCMS is first of all a spiritual community. We are drawn together by the Triune God, and for one ultimate purpose: that the knowledge of the glory of the Lord would saturate every corner of the world just as the waters cover the seas. If we are to make any contribution of eternal value, if we are to participate in this calling then we must seek intimacy with Him at all times. We fail, but the blood of Christ covers us and the grace of God through the eternal Spirit renews our spirits. Our first strategic priority calls us to be: *A strong, dynamic spiritual community characterised by faith, confidence in and dependence on the Triune God, passion for Christ and His Kingdom, and love for those within and outside OCMS.* As the Apostle Paul reminds us, Christ is the treasure chest of all God's wisdom and knowledge (Col 2:3). Our discovery of 'new knowledge' is simply the discovery of what God already knows. Therefore, our research and scholarship, if it is valid, will lead us to Christ, and our intimacy with God will lead us to his life-giving knowledge.

This journey of intimacy is not solely an individual one. The centre of OCMS life is our weekly Wednesday Chapel. Our other times of prayer, reflection on the Word and intercession are also vital. Our shared spiritual life and unity is the ground from which we live as third space and thick space. We have the privilege of working in a building that has been a place of worship for one hundred and sixty years. Can we not ask God to make this a thin space, a place of encounter with God where heaven and earth meet? On a number of occasions, visitors to OCMS have commented to me on the spirit within the team and sense of God's presence. We do not take this for granted. Just as we are intentional in seeking excellence in our work, so we must remain intentional in building a spiritual community. As we do, God will lead, strengthen and resource us in our calling to research and scholarship for the transformation of understanding, and participation in his mission so that one day, the earth will be filled with the knowledge of the glory of God as the waters cover the seas.

